AFTER ALL

Don Cupitt

AFTER ALL

Religion without Alienation

SCM PRESS LTD

0 334 00036 X

First published 1994
by SCM Press Ltd
26–30 Tottenham Road, London N1 4BZ

Typeset by Regent Typesetting, London
Printed and bound in Great Britain by
Biddles Ltd, Guildford and King's Lynn

Contents

for Susan

Introduction

Here's a paradox: the cultural resources and the wealth of knowledge about everything that are freely available to us today are far greater than ever before – and yet most people live in a fog. The culture has no common core, no spine any more. Indeed, it is very disorderly. We haven't got any unifying, reasonably rational and communally-held vision of life such as philosophy and religious belief once set out to provide. We have instead become information junkies who know everything, and therefore nothing.

The sort of world-view we have lost commonly took the form of an authoritative representation of the whole scheme of things and our place in it, laid out in a way that also showed us how we should live, towards what long-term goals our life should be directed, and what final good we might hope to attain. It thus fell into two main parts, *cosmos* and *ethos*, metaphysics and ethics, Creation and Redemption, but (more important) it held them together. If you wondered how human beings, who live not at the end of history but in its midst, and who occupy only one small corner of the whole, could hope to achieve such an overall vision of the human condition, religion and philosophy gave slightly different answers. Religion claimed that its teachings had been revealed by God, and philosophy held that there were objectively reliable and uncontaminated sources of knowledge, such as pure *a priori* reasoning, and the data of sense-experience. Reason in particular was a source of objective knowledge, because human reason was more than just human. It was our participation in an objective Order of Reason or Logos that pervaded all things. We could attain the god's eye-view, our thought could be godlike, because the human mind was made in the image of the divine Mind and could be illuminated by Eternal Reason.

Until the eighteenth century philosophy by and large maintained this theological conception of Reason, and while philosophy and theology remained closely allied Christendom held firm. But during the nineteenth century it was established beyond reasonable doubt that a human being is not an angel in a house of clay. We are merely clever animals who have invented knowledge in order to help ourselves to survive. The old belief that we could somehow rise above the limitations of our human senses and faculties, and see the human situation as if with God's own absolute and perspectiveless vision, finally broke down. We are always animals who live in time, we always see things from a standpoint inside our own human languages and cultures, and we are always conditioned by our place and historical period. Every philosophical system that tries to rise above these limits and achieve finality soon finds itself made into a quaint period piece just by the passage of time. In attempting a still representation of Reality as a whole we are like a person trying to draw the landscape as seen from a moving railway carriage. The great historicist systems of Hegel and Marx made huge efforts to incorporate and to take full account of historical change: but by a neat irony it has quickly, and in Hegel's case I think lethally, dated them too. Any philosophical system that attempts to incorporate history would be wise to remain unfinished.

What is more, during the nineteenth century there was a very rapid proliferation of new sciences, physical, biological, social and historical. Each became professionalized, setting out to create its own 'methodological community', a society of people committed to an agreed subject-matter, standard definitions of terms, agreed methods of working and agreed procedures for testing truth. Professionalization worked like a charm: knowledge grew at a prodigious rate, and the older metaphysical and religious belief-systems suddenly began to look windy, amateurish and primitive by comparison. Much genius had gone into constructing them, but they simply didn't meet the new standards. Were their terms clearly defined, did they have agreed methods of working, had they built up an agreed body of results, did they have agreed test-procedures for detecting and expunging errors? No, no, no, no.

By the end of the century metaphysics and systematic theology were dead in the water. Twentieth-century theology's concerns have subsequently been chiefly defensive: theology has worried about its response to biblical criticism, to the problem of evil, to secularization and to religious pluralism. It is at present impossible to imagine it reasserting its ancient sovereignty over all the newly-independent sciences and professions. It is said that when in 1979 Khomeini's followers took over in Iran they planned to reform and Islamize the intellectual content of such subjects as physics and medicine, which were taught in the country's Western-style universities. But how do you do it, what would it take, and what would be the cost? The project was shelved; and if even they in the moment of unfettered power were daunted, then we would be too. Old-style realistic systematic theology of the sort that prevailed for a thousand years after Augustine is no longer attempted by anyone. Not by Karl Barth, who rejected philosophy and limited himself to expounding the church's internal jargon. Barth's theology sounds very confident, but it is resonating inside an enclosed space that few now wish to enter.

Just by how much the old ambitions of theology have nowadays been given up is not often admitted; but in the case of philosophy there was an open revolt. Russell and Moore, for example, explicitly rejected large woolly edifying philosophy at the beginning of the century. It slipped away, and has never been fully reinstated. Philosophy may still be metaphysical in the sense of being revisionist. Ordinary language often seems to generate too complicated a world-picture, and philosophy may try to tidy things up by reducing mathematics to logic, the world to atomic facts, experience to sense-data, mind to behavioural skills and capacities, and so on. All that makes a lot of sense, for

3

many of the best modern knowledge-systems owe their success precisely to their determined effort to bring everything down to one level. Nowadays, surely, explanation has to be naturalistic. But by the same token modern philosophy must be opposed to metaphysics, if by metaphysics is meant the science that gives us access to some higher and hidden reality, truth or wisdom. The later Wittgenstein is a good exponent of the point here. Much though he had diverged from Russell in other ways, he still detested the flabby, useless language of large-scale Meaning-of-Life philosophy. 'Since everything lies open to view', he says, 'there is nothing to explain'.[1] It was enough to stay with the ways language is used in the most routine situations of everyday life. There, at least, what you hear seems to be intelligible, and there ought to be a chance of giving a purely-immanent explanation of it. And if we can achieve a transparent account of how language works on its home ground and in the most ordinary situations, then we'll be cured of metaphysics. We won't feel any need to think that life's wires are pulled from some point outside life, and we won't dream that there's an occult Answer to life's question hidden away somewhere Above. We won't even feel that there *is* a question.

So during the present century both philosophy and theology have largely dropped out of their former public role. Theology, presupposing faith and articulating the content of faith, is now internal to the church – or perhaps rather to a very small circle of people within the churches. Philosophy has become professionalized and academic. Neither philosophy nor theology can quite claim to be providing society as a whole with a coherent set of common-core convictions about how things are, how we should live, and in what direction we are together heading.

Does this matter? Not everyone thinks that either public life or private life should any longer be rooted in a shared worldview. Many have argued with Wittgenstein that no such set of common-core convictions is needed. They have held that it is sufficient to be uncommitted like an artist, or to live without ideology, or to seek happiness in love and work, or simply to immerse oneself in the present moment and in ordinariness.

Until recently I might have agreed with this. But there are one or two doubts. First, the end of metaphysics and the return of everything into ordinariness and the here and now is a great, and even a catastrophic, religious event. It is (arguably) tantamount to the end of the church and the coming of the Kingdom. It is the end of the old sacerdotal and other-worldly church-Christianity, and the arrival of a world in which 'organized religion' – that is, *alienated* religion – seems no longer to be needed. If Wittgenstein's work is done, if I am completely content with this, here, now, then I no longer need an authoritative Voice from Above to tell me 'Now, hear this!' I can live the Sermon on the Mount directly, because – as must already be obvious – Jesus was not a Christian, but a post-Christian. Post-Christianity, the Kingdom, preceded the church and will also succeed it.

A note about words is needed at this point. Recently, we have come to add the prefix 'post-' in cases where a cultural movement, by criticizing itself, has gone beyond itself into a different and more advanced state of itself. Post-modernism and post-feminism are examples. It is worth applying this notion to Christianity, because people often forget that the only sort of Christianity they have met, orthodox ecclesiastical Christianity, originally came into being as a second-best, and has always thought of itself as existing only for the sake of a greater reality yet to come, into which it hopes to pass over. This greater reality appears here and there under various names in Christian language. It is the Kingdom of God on earth, originally promised by Jesus. It is the Second Advent, the Millennium and Heaven. I'm using the term 'post-Christianity' by way of getting a new angle upon what this greater reality may be. The idea that our age is now post-philosophical and post-theological is associated especially with Heidegger. See, for example, *On Time and Being*, trans. Joan Stambaugh (Harper Torchbooks 1972). In the present text I want to keep some scraps of old vocabulary even while also trying to think in a new way.

The religious implications of this line of argument need to be explored; but there is also a second anxiety. If neither philosophy nor theology is reaching the public with a 'normal' and reasonably-rational picture of the human situation and the good life, then there is surely a danger of a spiritual vacuum. Do we not already see an enormous range of fundamentalisms, cults, fringe fads, nationalist excesses and whatnot rushing in to fill it? Again, until recently I would have said, 'Let a hundred flowers bloom'; but as the late-media society is succeeded by the information society I begin, as we all begin, to feel some doubts. The disorder, the excess, becomes unendurable.

Here is a paradox. A moment ago we described the religious optimism which sees the secular City as a fulfilment of biblical promise. Now we invoke the culture-pessimism of those who see it as Pandemonium. For some, our modern secular belieflessness and the decay of the old intellectual structures of Philosophy and theology is like the coming of the Kingdom of God; for others it is 'the time of the angels', when demons are abroad. How are we to arbitrate between these very-sharply conflicting responses to our present condition?

The answer I am proposing here is that although we *do* need something like a reinvention of metaphysics, it cannot take the form of a reinstatement of one of the old systems. The huge growth of modern knowledge has taken place, and cannot be reversed. But precisely because of that, we do need to come to terms with the now-extremely-detailed cosmic narrative offered by modern science. Has it wholly displaced the earlier cosmologies; and anyway, what's its status?

Secondly, one of the reasons for the proliferation of cults nowadays is that there are major fissures within the culture that we have developed. In particular, there's a split between the science-and-technology side of the culture, which is rationalistic and wants to bring everything down to numbers and to mathematical models of tiny scattering packets of energy, and the arts-and-communications side of the culture which wants to bring everything down to the mystery of language – not numbers, but ambiguous, elusive, tantalizing, signs-in-motion.

These are two excellent reductions, but they seem incompatible. Some sort of mediation between them is urgently needed. So in various places I have elsewhere suggested that a powerful metaphor might be a means of bridging the gap. The metaphor I proposed was that of a ripple moving across the surface of a pond, or, as it might be, a tremor moving across one of the sensory surfaces of the body.[2] The ripple is a sense-datum, or a sign. The underside of the ripple, down in the water-body, represents our feeling-response to an impingement upon a sense-organ, and it represents also the material 'body' of the sign. The upper surface of the ripple, in the air, represents the objective cultural world, and it represents also the public meaning of the sign. Around this metaphor I tried to build a text that would weave together the Word and the flesh, biological feeling and cultural meaning, into a continuous story.

The present suggestion, following up that idea, is that a new metaphysics might take the form of a network of such unifying metaphors. Not old-style pseudo-rigorous metaphysics, which was a fantasy, but just a network of metaphors; and not any sort of extra information about another realm, but just ways of connecting up things you already know. With the help of these metaphors we might be able to develop a very simple and clear picture of the world and the human situation. It will need to include an account of the scientific world-story, and to show what sort of status we should ascribe to it. With it will be associated accounts of ethics and of the forms that active and contemplative religion may take in the future.

In short, I'm attempting not a revival of old-style dogmatic metaphysics, but only a sketch – metaphorical, admittedly, but clear, as I hope – of the antirealist vision of life that follows the end of the old metaphysics and the old systematic theology. I'm asking what view of life is reasonable just now. I'm trying to describe a new sort of natural theology and natural religion, and ending by suggesting that in different parts of the world different faith-traditions may (if they wish) supplement it in various ways.

So, to repeat, I'm after a minimal creed, a post-postmodernist attempt at reconstruction, and I want it to be as simple and clear as possible. But there is a problem. Modern culture is so capacious that in one corner of the market the scientists are reciting their prodigious new Grand Narrative cosmology, in complete confidence that it will function in future as the story we will live by, and innocently unaware of the questions raised about all such stories by post-structuralist and post-modernist thought; while in the opposite corner of the market up-to-date literary and cultural theorists blithely take it for granted that all the Grand Narratives are dead, and that science may be disregarded anyway.

But we can't disregard the scientific world-story. It intrigues us, because it is so very odd. In the familiar narrative 'Man', the talkative primate, creeps on to the cosmic stage only at the very end of the story. So who's told the earlier chapters of the story, and from what authorial standpoint? Whose is this godlike intelligence that roams free across billions of light-years? Surely it can't belong to that poor chattering hairless ape that just slouched in? It seems inconceivable that the sign-vocabulary of this latest and least important of creatures should suddenly be able to go sweeping back and encompass the Big Bang and the birth of the galaxies.

To keep these difficulties out of sight, the scientific community requires in scientific papers a strict and systematic effacement of the personality of the author. In addition, scientists usually assume the perfect transparency of language, so that the observation that they are always operating inside their own natural and mathematical sign-systems does not seem to them to be worrying.

By these devices the problems are kept out of sight. But they remain real, and they present an obstacle to us, because to an arts person who cares about words language cannot be perfectly transparent. For the physicist, everything can be mathematically modelled, and everything happens in the cosmic space across which energies radiate and scatter. For the writer, everything happens in the weird multi-dimensional space of linguistic meaning. How are we to imagine the relation between these two sorts of space? How is one's nearest and dearest able to be both a flesh-and-blood animal like oneself, and a person, a communicator, a positive fountain of signs? How can the space of the body be also the space of linguistic meaning?

8

How can *science* take the linguistic turn? A far-fetched question, which shows why it is hard to be quite as simple as I'd like to be about the present human situation and its religious possibilities. But we'll do our best. We need to try, I'm suggesting, because if it is true that we can no longer hope to frame reasonable common-core conceptions of the world, the self and the good that people might agree to share, then there must be a danger that the culture will be entirely dissolved away by the flood of infotainment technologies.

I need to deal with the scientific world-picture because I am that very unusual sort of animal, an antirealist who loves science. I shall suggest that an antirealist view of science has religious possibilities. And I'm also suggesting a certain convergence between post-Christianity and post-philosophy. The old theology, in alliance with platonism, posited two worlds – this world, and a Better World above, which was also a World to Come. Nowadays we find that both philosophy and theology want to posit only one world. It seems a straightforward ambition, but the philosophical difficulties have proved great. Postmodernism was a mood of doubt about whether any reasonably stable and coherent world-picture could be formed at all. Here I shall suggest a new role for religious thought: to propose unifying and totalizing metaphors which will help us to view the world as a field on which the religious life can be lived. I call such a world 'the Kingdom', alluding to the ancient hope that one day the state of religious alienation will come to an end.

Why the philosophical difficulties? Looking back, I think that during the eighties I underestimated the difficulty of explaining what the old realism in philosophy and theology amounted to, why it has broken down, and how we can learn to be happier without it. Realism envisaged the Universe as a great *institution*, class society on a cosmic scale, disciplinary, hierarchically-ordered, with a modest place prepared for you and expectations about your behaviour.[3] People love that, and will not readily give it up. When you live in an institution you know where you belong and what is required of you. Outside it, you would feel utterly lost and disoriented.

9

Today, we feel disoriented because the church has in the past identified itself so completely with the realistic vision of the Universe. It was too paradoxical of me to suggest that the church could and should move out of her old and now-decaying world-picture, and learn instead to live by a non-realist interpretation of her faith. In fact, as church leaders know well, ecclesiastical Christianity is realistic by definition. Talk about the end of realism is in effect talk about the end of ecclesiastical Christianity and the arrival of post-Christianity. One would scarcely expect church leaders to be enthusiastic about *that*.

Yet, ironically, by their own lights they ought to welcome the end of the church. For as they know, the church only came into being in the first place as a temporary stop-gap and a second-best. Jesus had originally preached the Kingdom, and the Kingdom was not at all a lowly state of exile from a better world Above: the Kingdom was itself to be a condition of final and unsurpassable fulfilment, on this earth. But because the promised Kingdom had failed to arrive, the church developed to maintain order in the interim.

That's why the church is realist through and through. The church is based on the idea that the Kingdom is infinitely postponed, but still promised. Meanwhile, our present state of existence is very imperfect, but only transitory. Doctrine is needed, to tell us on good authority that a better world is to come; and a disciplinary structure and sacraments are needed, because we are on probation and must purify ourselves in preparation for the New Age. In the church, as in other faiths, the task of priests and other religious professionals is to mediate between this world and the spiritual world. They have a vested interest in maintaining the condition of religious alienation, because they make their livelihood out of it. So as the church settled down in time, and the Kingdom receded into the future, the better state of things for which we are preparing came to be identified with life after death. Thus the church allied itself with Platonism, and with the state. It became radically committed to realism and to a pessimistic view of the human condition in this life. We are servants, who live by standards and obey orders that come down from the mysterious realm Upstairs: but life outside the Household of Faith would be so dreadful that we are very fortunate to have our place here in it.

In talking about the end of theological realism, I was trying to break with Christianity's historic pessimism and other-worldliness. For all sorts of scientific reasons, it is time to decide that there is nothing wrong with the senses, the body, this world, time and this life, and there is nothing wrong with the standards and values that we have ourselves developed. It is time to give up the old sense of exile, and the metaphysics that *defers* all value and all true happiness to a higher and invisible Realm above. We want a quite new kind of Kingdom-religion, grown-up, open-air and free-moving. It is time to leave the world of 'service'.

But of course I underestimated the fierceness of people's attachment to realism, which has after all been the dominant mode of thought for two-and-a-half millennia; and I found it hard myself to grasp the implications of what I was saying. When we are talking about the end of old-style realistic philo-sophy and theology, when we are talking about the antirealist vision of life, what are we talking about – *Götterdämmerung*, or the Kingdom? It is time for a new effort to catch up with ourselves and see where the argument has by now brought us.

The American death-of-God theologian T. J. J. Altizer points out in a recent book[4] that the death of God coincided with the invention of the footnote – in Bentley's *Milton*, in fact. At that moment language lost its old divine authority and truth began to depend upon a mere human consensus. Instead of the old glorious rhetoric and the strong poetry of which Milton had been one of the last exponents, writers were reduced to invoking a boring procession of academic expert witnesses to testify in support of what they said.

Keen to renew religious thought, Altizer promised to do with-out footnotes. He didn't quite keep his promise, and in any case I don't promise to imitate his rhetorical style. Instead, I have cut down severely on the footnotes, and I follow Kierkegaard in disclaiming any authority at all, whether divine or academic. This book is not the Truth: but at least it *is* true, for now. I thank John Drury and Hugh Rayment-Pickard for their comments on and criticisms of a draft version of it.

D.C.

1

The Emergence of Post-Christianity

Post-Christianity is a new religious reality, which has been developing unrecognized over the past fifteen years or so. Now it has reached the point where it needs to be described and to become more conscious of itself.

It is not and cannot be entirely new. Recent debate has suggested that post-modernism may be older than modernism, and in the same way the sort of radically post-traditional kind of religion that I am going to describe may have preceded traditional religious belief.

A vivid example of this comes from the critic Harold Bloom, who is unusual amongst today's literary theorists in his fascination with the question of authorship. Jewish himself, and a lover of great epic writing, Bloom has written with particular enthusiasm about the J-narrative which has been disentangled from the earliest books of the Bible.[1] The J-narrative is, so far as we know, the founding epic of God. It established the literary personality of Yahweh/Jehovah, an overwhelmingly dominant figure, a demanding, persecuting, jealous, capricious, enthralling super-male Ego. He is probably the single most stupendous and widely-influential literary personality ever created, remaining to this day a major psychic fact for half the human race. When people say they believe in God, they are testifying to the continuing influence upon them of the literary personality created by the unknown author of J. For twenty-five years I disliked Freud for saying that the God of philosophical theism is negligible, whereas the imperious abrupt Yahweh is real and important. Now I see, as Bloom sees, that Freud was correct. And Bloom is fascinated by the thought of the writer who invented God, the writer who had to be the strongest poet of them all.

Bloom thinks it poetically apt that the (slightly-mocking) creator of the ultimate male ego should have been a woman; but that is by the way. Within a very few centuries, J's achievement had become ingested into and normalized within a developing tradition. Traditionalization involves scriptures, and therefore scribes; a cult, and therefore priests; a communally-held orthodoxy, and therefore the quenching of the spirit of strong poetry. In the New Testament God has nothing fresh to say: the only phrases ascribed to him are quotes from his own younger and more vital self, and his very Name, Yahweh, is no longer spoken. *Ichabod*: the glory has departed.

However, the de-traditionalization of religion in the modern period has gradually dismantled block-orthodoxy and the block-view of scripture. We have learned how the tradition was first put together and slowly became hallowed. Fine: but more important is the awesome realization that language once had the pure creative religious power and force apparent in the oldest biblical narratives. Indeed the entire body of Holy Tradition, which seems so real and coherent, so grand and timeless, and so thickly-populated with superhuman beings, is a purely contingent human accumulation. We made it all up! Post-traditional and post-ecclesiastical Christianity, moving out of the fading world of tradition, seeks to re-awaken the spirit of strong poetry. My God – writing once had the power to create God! So we move away from the idea of religion as obedient conformity and the endless recycling of an unchanging tradition, and try to learn instead to trust the true Creator of all things, the religious imagination.

Post-Christianity may thus find a pedigree of sorts in the great tradition of strong epic poetry from J and Job to Blake and Joyce. Bloom knows, and Altizer amongst the theologians knows, that strong poetry doesn't just respectfully copy the way things are. It creates: it makes and unmakes the very gods themselves. It is the Sacred, a power which is beyond good and evil.

However, a more proximate factor in the current emergence of post-Christianity is to be sought in the way that modern philosophy and theology have developed. In the history of ideas in the West the crucial period was around 1775 to 1845.

In philosophy, Hume's *Dialogues* (posthumously published 1779) and Kant's *Critique of Pure Reason* (1781) successfully brought to an end the old notion that our thinking could altogether outsoar the world of experience and attain to a higher world of eternal Reality. Since then, the ideas of a metaphysical god and an immortal human soul have never been reinstated in their traditional form. Fichte's dismissal from his Jena professorship for atheism took place in 1799. Hegel saved his own academic career by enhistorizing both God and the old objective order of Reason. God became Progress, God became History, God became Western Culture's movement towards absolute knowledge. Schopenhauer followed Kant, heard Fichte, and disliked Hegel's temporizing. He became the first avowed atheist amongst the German philosophers (*The World as Will and as Representation*, 1818). By the 1840s the Young Hegelians, who included Feuerbach and Marx, were increasingly committed to atheism and radical humanism.

News of these developments reached even England, where writers of the generation of Thomas Carlyle, J. A. Froude and George Eliot recognized what was happening. At the same time a new theological crisis developed. It had been known, at least since the time of Isaac Le Peyrère and Spinoza in the seventeenth century, that biblical criticism could present a major threat to revealed theology. Locke and Newton, who were (unlike the Deists) capable and highly-regarded figures, both understood very clearly that the two great dogmas of orthodox ecclesiastical Christianity, the Trinity and the incarnation, are not quite scriptural. Only these two dogmas were ever fully defined by the undivided church – and it got them both wrong. This opened a very large crack in the foundations of traditional Christianity, but the power of the church remained great enough to paper it over until the early nineteenth century.

The key book is doubtless still D. F. Strauss's *Life of Jesus*

(1835–6), to be taken with perhaps just the title of a short work of 1865, *The Christ of Faith and the Jesus of History.* Strauss established permanently a sharp distinction between an original Jewish Jesus, witnessed to in the Gospels of Matthew, Mark and Luke and believed by some to be the (human) Messiah, and the co-eternal Son or Word of God of John's Gospel and the developed metaphysical dogma of the Gentile church. Strauss seems also to have fixed in our heads the thought that the development from the former to the latter may be explained in terms of the workings of the human mythopoeic imagination.

Strauss directed much of his polemic against F.D.E. Schleiermacher (1768–1834), who was one of the very last considerable defenders of ecclesiastical Christianity. But I am suggesting that Strauss's argument may be seen as having done two jobs at once: it destroyed ecclesiastical Christianity indeed, but it also opened the way to post-Christianity. Strauss's mythical interpretation (as he called it) showed how the entire christological epic narrative, the cosmic drama of salvation built up by Paul, Irenaeus and Augustine, might be viewed as the product of the mythopoeic imagination; and so indirectly Strauss revealed how prodigiously powerful a force the religious imagination can be. Our human world is everywhere and outsidelessly temporal, language-formed and *therefore* a flux of narratives. We are always inside several rolling stories at once. But the greatest stories, those that make the most sense of their lives to most people for the longest periods, are usually the epic narratives of religion. One day we may come to see Charles Darwin as having told such a story – and perhaps one of the greatest.

To resume our main argument, which is about why post-Christianity is emerging just now, we have seen that by the 1840s the main intellectual claims of ecclesiastical Christianity had finally collapsed. The existence of God cannot be proved, and, looking back, we are hard put to it to say whether a single major thinker since the Middle Ages has been able to do anything to make the idea of life after death either plausible or even intelligible. Our world is the human world, a world bounded by language, time and narrativity, and radically outsideless. All this is all there is. This is it. We have no reason to speak either of a metaphysical 'soul' on this side of the flux of language-formed events, or of any metaphysical Reality out there on the far side of the flux of language-formed events. The flux is outsideless. There is only all this, and there's nothing wrong with all this. The work of religion ought to be, not to take us out of it, but simply to reconcile us to it. So the old 'realistic' or metaphysical ideas of God, the soul and life after death are now untenable: or, to put the point a little more cautiously, they cannot now be *proved* in the way that until the eighteenth century it was thought they could be. And, indeed, old-style dogmatic Philosophy in the tradition founded by Plato has already largely given way to post-philosophy.

Furthermore, the grand dogmas of historic ecclesiastical Christianity are not strictly scriptural. Those who continue to claim that there is a point-by-point scriptural justification for their doctrines can easily be shown point-by-point that there is not. The best that can be said is that Western Christianity's great doctrinal epic is a strange and splendid *midrash*, a work of art, a very detailed romance loosely based upon the Bible. At many points it has become very obscure to us, because it reflects lost ways of thinking. The doctrines of the Trinity and the incarnation, of Christ's atoning death and his resurrection, have become so opaque that no theologian since the Enlightenment has been able to spell out what they are supposed to mean in a way that is intellectually coherent, morally acceptable, and moderately plausible, whilst at the same time being acceptable to the faithful as an articulation of what they believe themselves to believe.

These things are known to every beginner in the study of theology, and have been known for around a century. Because they wish to retain a shred of intellectual credibility, the churches still require ministerial candidates to study some theology, but advise them that the study of theology will test their faith. It will indeed, and after they are ordained they quickly and prudently forget all about theology. Having learned its dangers, they are now inoculated for life against any further infection from that quarter.

A wide consensus has thus developed, especially since the 1840s or so, that faith is non-rational. One believes because it seems to be one's duty to believe, upon the authority of the Pope, or tradition, or the Bible, or on the basis of personal 'experience', and one is most wary of permitting mere secular reason to erode away something so precious. *Credo quia absurdum*: it seems that a touch of irrationality lends spice to faith. A merely rational religion would be boring. The church demonstrates its own numinous power by its ability to make us believe absurdities. And we? – yes, it seems that we want to be manipulated into taking untruths for our truths. Every believer nowadays is a half-conscious Nietzschean: our truths are those illusions without which we cannot live, the illusions we have fallen in love with and want to be made to believe.

Although many people thus find religious authoritarianism highly attractive, it still needs to be maintained by sociological pressures. These have become stronger and stronger recently. In the Roman Catholic Church, since the proclamation of Papal infallibility in 1870 and the introduction of the Anti-Modernist Oath in 1910, it has been made clear that the most rigorous intellectual discipline is to be applied to the clergy. (In the purge of the Modernists many priests were excommunicated: laypeople were disregarded.) During the pontificate of the present Pope, John-Paul II, the pressure upon priest-theologians with a *missio canonica*, operating in seminaries or in faculties of Catholic theology, has become intolerable to honest people, and there have been many, many distinguished casualties.

The other area in which we now find traditional ecclesiastical faith being defended by strong sociological pressures is within conservative protestantism, especially in the English-speaking world, and especially in the USA, where this type of religion has a long history. Modern 'fundamentalism' is usually dated from the controversies of 1918-31. Its opposition to darwinism, biblical criticism and modern liberalism has continued, and now takes a highly political form which poses a real threat to the teaching of biology in schools and to the humane practice of medicine. The extreme anti-intellectualism of the Evangelicals is very baffling, because it shows how social pressures can somehow create meaning. Evangelical religious language appears to be quite intelligible to insiders, but makes no sense at all to outsiders. Equally perplexing is the moral absolutism of the religious Right. A new kind of moral fundamentalism is abroad, and we have already seen the first deaths of hunt saboteurs (in England) and of abortion clinic doctors (in the USA).

In summary, a modernization of ecclesiastical faith might still have been possible as late as 1820 or so. At that time Hegel and Schleiermacher were the very last front-rank thinkers who were also comfortable practising churchmen. Their work suggested the possibility of revising away the old supernaturalism; but the chance was missed and by the 1840s it was too late. The chief intellectual claims of faith were damaged, as it has turned out, beyond repair. The churches became committed to a long rearguard action in defence of tradition against modernity. As their decline has slowly accelerated their irrationalism has grown more extreme. Their language has deteriorated, and their internal life has become more disorderly.

The resulting situation has become very difficult for the churches. Since the 1840s, traditional apologetics has broken down. Faith just cannot prove its own rationality. Everyone tacitly concedes now that religious belief is non-rational, and many are actively in favour of irrationality. So orthodox faith comes to be held in place by appeals to authority and by sociological pressures. But these measures cannot work for long. Without intellectual anchorage, religious language sounds vapid and ineffectual. It spins uselessly without doing any real work, like a cog that turns but doesn't engage with anything. And the long-term results are entirely predictable: delirium, the breakdown of discipline, disorder and anarchy. Because it is so insecure, faith begins to show the mixture of sentimentality and vindictiveness that Nietzsche has described so well.

In this climate theologians find themselves perceived as being at best useless, and at worst a threat. How are they to justify their tenure of posts in publicly-funded institutions, when it has become so hard to claim that any of the beliefs which are held in the churches are part of the common stock of public knowledge?

The American separation of church and state suggests one solution. Theology splits into two rather different subjects. Seminary theology is tied to the funding denomination. It scarcely makes larger intellectual claims: it concentrates on communicating the paymaster denomination's traditions and culture to students for the ministry, and teaches them 'pastoral theology' – i.e., the gentle art of running a church that makes a healthy profit. The other kind of theology, found in University Departments of Religion, aims at academic respectability and is therefore not ecclesiastical. It chiefly pursues critical study of the history of religions, the idea being that facts about religion, established by the application to publicly-available data of a publicly-recognized intellectual method, can surely be part of the common stock of public knowledge. So that's agreed – but it is also tacitly agreed that religious beliefs themselves somehow cannot any longer be established and made part of common knowledge.

This is a dire situation. True, a few energetic individuals find loopholes, and contrive to do publicly interesting work in the philosophy of religion and in creative religious thought. But they are likely to be laypeople and post-Christians. Everywhere today the propositions of ecclesiastical faith have irretrievably lost public significance, even as church discipline still struggles to hold on to them. Some people hope that, even though religious Objects have faded, they may still derive comfort 'from their religious beliefs', as the idiom has it. They are hoping to be saved just by their own religious feelings. But privatized and non-rational faith gradually loses the power to give comfort in adversity.

Historic, ecclesiastical Christianity laid great emphasis upon correct credal belief, upon submission to its authority-structure and its discipline, and upon exclusive communion. So long as all this could be rationally justified, it was tolerable. What is rational is catholic and objective, and will lift you up above your local ethnic preoccupations and concerns. But when rationality was lost, the universal dimension was lost. Your people's religious beliefs became just a part of the stock of fundamental and pre-rational shared assumptions that is your people's cultural heritage. Your old exclusive allegiance to the church universal now becomes exclusive ethnocentricity. It leads you to reach for a machine-gun – and your subsequent attitudes and behaviour will be very much the same whether you are a Sikh, a Serb, a Zionist, an Armenian, a Muslim Brotherhood member, a Hindu militant or whatever. Just *what* you believe makes no difference; but *that* you believe is all important and is indeed all you have got left.

All this follows from the sad fact that no religion (or philosophy) today has the sort of catholic rationality that Western science and technology have got. The pressures that are leading many Christian theologians and writers to move into post-Christianity are felt in other faiths too. Perhaps if it is to become truly a world-faith Christianity will have to go beyond itself into post-Christianity; but in making that move it must expect to find itself converging with refugees from other religious traditions. *And* taking science seriously, too.

Today's post-Christianity is thus being experienced as a religious liberation. Since the mid-nineteenth century, people who have outgrown ecclesiastical Christianity have tended to think of themselves as 'lapsed', as 'agnostics' or 'humanists'. They have sounded as if they feel themselves diminished – orphaned by the death of God, and alienated from Mother Church.

Even Bishop John Robinson could still use the metaphor of feeling orphaned.[2] But today's post-Christianity sees no reason whatever to describe itself in such romantically pessimistic terms. On the contrary, it regards its own appearance as evidence that traditional ecclesiastical Christianity has now completed its historical task, which always was in the end to go beyond itself, exceed itself and become something greater than itself.

The notion that 'organized religion', ecclesiastical Christianity, is only a temporary arrangement takes a variety of forms, ancient and modern. The original Jewish hope was for the coming of the Kingdom of God, and the Kingdom was not a form of organized religion. In it the sacrificial system and the mediation of religion through sacred objects, ordinances, structures of authority and the like were expected to disappear.

Jesus himself is accordingly depicted in the Synoptic Gospels as living a Kingdom-life and teaching a Kingdom-ethic. He appears, irregularly, at Temple or synagogue – but only, it seems, in order to teach, prophesy or otherwise engage in controversy. He does not join in public worship. When he prays, he prays alone, or with his friends. He is not a religious professional. In terms of the Weberian contrast between charismatic and institutional religion, he is shown as highly charismatic, cheerfully overriding or disregarding rank, law, tradition and taboo as and when it suits him.

The full arrival of the Kingdom being delayed, the structures of organized religion are depicted in the New Testament as having begun to evolve, in a very haphazard way, only *after* Jesus' death. (He did not 'found' them.) They include such things as Sunday assemblies for worship, a recognized leadership which may on occasion meet in council and lay down rules, a very simple profession of faith, and sacraments. All such structures have the purpose of ordering the community's life during the interim period while the Lord's return is awaited. When he comes, they must disappear.

Thus the entire apparatus of organized religion was originally seen as having a disciplinary function, and was a symptom of alienation. The believer's notion of an objective God, in a heavenly world to which Jesus the Messiah-designate had been temporarily withdrawn, seemed appropriate during the time of waiting. But when Christ returned to earth and the Kingdom was established, all the objective structures of religion would disappear. In the final vision of the heavenly city at the end of the book of Revelation, at the end of Dante's *Divine Comedy*, in Jan van Eyck's Ghent altarpiece, and at the end of the *Pilgrim's Progress*, there is no Temple and God is not seen as a distinct object. Rather God is dispersed into a light, or Glory, that irradiates everything and everyone. In my own former terminology, the End is non-realistic. Even the tradition knew *that*.

So in post-Christianity too there are no longer two worlds but only one – *this* world; and there is no longer an objective God, but only a general confusion and merging together of the sacred and the profane. Everything that lives is holy. You want it now? – you can have it now.

Amongst early modern post-Christian writers, L.A. Feuerbach (*The Essence of Christianity*, 1841) shows an excellent grasp of these points. Ancient religion tended to project the divine out into objectivity, and so left Christianity with the historical task of returning the divine into the human. The return of God into humanity happens in the incarnation, in the mystical tradition, in the touching religious humanism of the later Middle Ages, in the Protestant Reformation, and in the rise of modern humanism. So ecclesiastical Christianity's job is done when the divine has become fully resolved down into the human. This resolves *agape* down into *eros*, making Feuerbach one of the first philosophers to assign high value to sex. Through heterosexual love we can pursue personal development, and indeed seek to be united with the universal human (i.e., God) in the person of the partner of the opposite sex.

No such sentiments, though, from Albert Schweitzer. In Schweitzer's version, the historical task of ecclesiastical Christianity is progressively to work itself out of a job – indeed, very precisely, to *de-skill* itself – as one by one it takes the elements of the future world and deliberately anticipates them, bringing them forward into the present age. Schweitzer sees Paul as already thinking in these terms. Through his death, Jesus had 'brought to an end the dominion of the powers of evil in the world, and set in motion the process, shown in his resurrection,

of transforming the natural world into the supernatural'.[3]
The de-skilling happens because the more the two worlds are
amalgamated, the less need there is for the old priestly skill
of managing communication between them.

Other features of the world to come which were appropriated
in the first generation or so included the open publication
of the secret of Jesus' messiahship, the forgiveness of sins, the
outpouring of the Spirit, the living of a risen and ascended life
'in Christ', and the reception of various charismatic gifts. As the
writer to the Hebrews puts it (6.5), 'We have tasted ... the
powers of the age to come'.

The Kingdom was also supposed to be an era of fertility and
prosperity, but for over a millennium Christian culture took
a pessimistic view of this life. However, with the Renaissance
and the scientific revolution Schweitzer sees a new spirit
of 'ethical world-affirmation' spreading, as it comes to be
thought that nature is law-governed, intelligible and amenable
to human control. For Schweitzer the prosperity of the modern
world, which crazies call 'materialism', was *also* a sign of the
Kingdom. The chief remaining problem is universal peace,
a promised feature of the Kingdom which we are as yet very far
from anticipating successfully.

For Schweitzer, then, what counts is world-affirmation,
reverence for life, the ethics of love and world peace. In so
far as we can realize these ideas generally, we have built
the Kingdom of God on earth and church-Christianity becomes
redundant. And Schweitzer – consistently with his general
outlook and his life's work – was of course a metaphysical
atheist who did not believe in any supernatural dogmas at all.
He just believed in Jesus and the Kingdom, and he wanted to see
Christianity urgently complete its historical task and vanish
into its true successor-faith – which he called the Kingdom and
I'm calling post-Christianity.

Both Feuerbach and Schweitzer were doubtless somewhat
influenced by Hegel in their suggestion that within history, and
by a purely immanent process of historical development, the
church is already completing its task and going beyond itself

into the Kingdom. Both were metaphysical atheists, and both in effect equated the Kingdom with a universal this-worldly religious humanism of love and reconciliation. I'm invoking both as harbingers of our own experience of post-Christianity.

To this two sharp retorts will be made. It will be said in the first place that Jesus was theocentric and preached the coming of the Kingdom *of God*. To this I can reply that Jesus' Kingdom seems almost to have been a Kingdom without a King. He refuses to be himself its King-Messiah, and in fact is extremely wary of speaking of God as King.[4] Jesus avoids doctrinal teaching about either God or the Kingdom. The Kingdom is a coming moral order and religious condition of which one speaks obliquely and in parables. To teach a doctrine of it would be to reintroduce precisely the sort of alienating religious ideology and structures that Jesus is seeking to get rid of. Yes: he works to free us from everything that the church became. As others have noticed, the post-Modern, post-Christian age is an age when people can live without ideology. We don't need it any longer.

Jesus *can* therefore be seen as a prophet of post-Christianity. The second objection is that the church was traditionally believed to be indefectible. It will be preserved, and preserved in the true Faith, until the End of history. Thus the final transition from church to Kingdom, and from ecclesiastical Christianity to post-Christianity, can be brought about only by supernatural agency and at the End of historical time. It cannot happen within history as we are claiming, but only after history. Schweitzer himself admits the difficulty, of course, but doesn't explain how it is that through human agency not only 'the powers of the age to come', but also the Age to Come *itself* can be brought forward and made to happen within history.

My reply to this objection is that the transition from Christianity to post-Christianity is part of the transition from modernism to post-modernism, which in a certain sense is indeed occurring at the End of history, for it brings to an end a certain conception of what history is.

Modernism was marked by a very strong belief in progressive

historical development through linear time towards a final liberation of humanity at the end of history. We were to bring all this about by a constant effort at self-overcoming. By systematic criticism of our knowledge and our institutions we were to strive steadily to increase our knowledge and to rationalize our world. The imagery was all of improvement, progress, advance and marching. The most interesting and significant human beings are those in the vanguard, those at the leading edge. They are in tune with the *Zeitgeist*; they are where it's at. Kierkegaard amusingly speaks of the reading of the daily newspaper over his breakfast as the morning devotions of modern man. Through the paper he communes with the *Zeitgeist*, at the leading edge of world-historical development.

In its faith in the possibility of historical progress through criticism of the present order of things and constant striving for betterment, Modernism is reminiscent of some strands in Calvinist thought. Indeed, the two traditions were actually amalgamated in American culture. Under the Providence of God, and guided by his Spirit, citizens of the New World were to build the Kingdom of God in America, repenting of and criticizing present reality and striving for the progressive realization of religious values in personal and social life.

But suppose Modernism in its zeal for self-criticism and self-overcoming should finally get around to criticizing its own mythology? For there is a glaring paradox in the Modernist programme, which we can view as lurking in the phrase 'to achieve progress'. For to *achieve* progress we must in principle regard everything, but everything, as open to criticism and reform; but to know that it is *progress* we have achieved something must have been left untouched, namely the criterion of progress itself.

Once we have understood that paradox, others multiply uncontrollably. For example: to effect change, the *avant garde* must be transgressive; but when (as in corporate America) progressive improvement becomes orthodoxy, the *avant garde* becomes the Establishment. And at the End of history Modernism pictures us as being fully and finally liberated, i.e.

free, in a world completely rationalized, planned and managed on the basis of total knowledge and therefore *not* free.

The emerging paradoxes of Modernism thus tip it over into post-Modernism, a curious state of affairs in which the Modernist paradoxes are not resolved but oddly entrenched. We postmoderns live in a queer sort of history after the end of History, precisely because we have recently seen through Reason and progressed beyond the belief in progress. We are trying to get used to living without any form at all of the old belief in 'one far-off divine event, to which the whole creation moves'. We recognize the irrationality of dreaming that if our social life were completely rationalized we'd all be freer and happier. We recognize that for a temporal, striving being, complete rational consistency is never quite attainable. And so on, for post-Modernism is still a Modernism. It is hyperbolic Modernism, which by thoroughly criticizing and demythologizing itself has exceeded itself and gone beyond even itself.

And by the same token, post-Christianity is still a Christianity. As both Nietzsche and Schweitzer already recognized a century ago, Christianity contains within itself an impulse to self-criticism which has led it since the Enlightenment progressively to demythologize itself. At the completion of the process, in about 1980, ecclesiastical Christianity tipped over into post-Christianity in just the same way as Modernism had already tipped over into post-Modernism. And we will also see Philosophy tipping itself over into post-philosophy.

2

The Death of Tradition

In every society, including our own, there are traditionalists, people who insist that all would be well with us if only we would stick fast to our traditional customs, beliefs and values. Such people are liable to forget that the notion of tradition is morally ambiguous.

In particular, any act of tradition may turn out to have been an act of betrayal. In Latin, a *traditio* is a handover, as when in early Christianity the teaching of the creed to a convert was called the *traditio symboli*. But the words treason, traitor and betrayal also come from the same root. The ambiguity is preserved in all Romance languages, and most noticeably in Italian. It is also made much of in the New Testament, where the word *paradosis* (giving up, handing down) is used both for the delivery of Jesus into the hands of his enemies and for the transmission of the faith ('the tradition of sound doctrine') in the church. And Jesus himself frequently attacks religious traditions as transgressions (Mark 7.9–13 etc.).

But, furthermore, historians have written much recently about 'the invention of tradition', especially in nineteenth-century England. In this department, one suspects, the Victorians were in a sense already postmoderns like us. They loved dressing up and playing games very seriously; and they played at fictioning a theme-park Heritage England, very much as we do. 'From now on ...' we begin, and we institute a new tradition. It is, as everyone knows, just a game, whose rules get their authority solely from people's consent to them. We enjoy playing it, so we accept the rules.

Thus a tradition may be – and often is – a betrayal, or

a transgression, or just a game. But there is also another and very much more serious sense of tradition: the sense in which it governs the way we see the world and produces the reality of religious objects.

Thus in Ireland it is possible for the Blessed Virgin Mary to become a real person. The complex and slowly-evolved cult of Mary can have such an effect upon the imagination of country girls that it makes her real. They see her, and hear her speak.

In the Southern USA amongst twice-born Protestants it is similarly possible for Jesus to become a real person with whom one communes each morning. He speaks, but is not usually seen. He is produced as an objective reality by the group's traditionally-evolved beliefs about him and devotion to him.

Interestingly, the *human* Jesus, intuited by feeling as a really-existing object of devotion present to the individual believer, first came into existence only quite recently. Classical Christianity was theocentric, and its high-class mysticism followed the platonic style of piety. There was no question of having another quasi-human person in your head. The divine Christ Almighty (*pantocrator*), seated at God's right hand and scheduled to be the universal Judge, was too fearsome a figure to be the object of an ordinary person's personal devotion. Accordingly, direct prayer to the human Jesus on the part of an ordinary believer is exceedingly rare before the seventeenth century. At that time piety becomes more Jesucentric amongst certain Jesuits and English Puritans, and in France.[1] This new Jesucentric piety was democratized by Pietists and early Methodists. It was taken to America, where it has flourished.

These things evolve slowly and are hard to judge from the texts. But, give or take a few decades either way, the Jesus of the Evangelical preacher thus came into existence around 1630 or so. Could you tell the preacher that? No, of course not.

Mary, as Catholic girls now see her, came into being much earlier – in the high Middle Ages, or even around 350 or so, it seems. But of course to their devotees Jesus and Mary are real persons, who have presumably been available to piety ever since their respective assumptions into Heaven.

But what *is* their objective reality as the believer experiences it? Despite the apparitions, it is clearly not exactly of the everyday empirical kind. It is the special reality of religious objects, which is produced by the local tradition, posited by faith and confirmed in personal experience. And there is no doubt at all that the believer insists upon a highly realistic vocabulary, and will not be budged from it. In an untouched traditional society, prior to the impact of Enlightenment and modernity, tradition creates a whole complex world for believers – a world of divine beings, angels, saints, demons, departed souls and good and evil powers and influences. And it is all real.

A possible and interesting exception to this general equation of traditionalism and realism is the Anglo-Catholic believer. Being Victorians at heart, Anglo-Catholics also greatly enjoy dressing-up and playing games with a straight face. Their 'ritualism' is rather consciously *naughty*, camp and ironical. Naturally they do not care to be 'straight'. They are dissidents, and what they privately are and think must remain unsaid. But their behaviour has always suggested the aptness of a radical symbolist or non-realist interpretation of their piety. The same might be said of many of the grander sort of Roman prelates from the sixteenth to nineteenth centuries.

For ordinary Roman Catholics and twice-born Protestants, though, the religious object has just got to be objectively real – which means that our modern critical and historical ways of thinking will in the long run destroy their faith. Modernity introduces rapid cultural change, which must weaken tradition. Further, the new ways of thinking work relentlessly to persuade us to accept that our tradition, which we had thought went back to the Origin and was somehow natural, is after all only a local and historically-evolved point of view. Worse still, critical thinking gradually insinuates the vital idea that the reality of the religious object, which we naïvely believed was *given* to us in and through our experience, was in fact merely *projected into* our experience by ourselves under the guidance of tradition.

Tradition creates reality. It shapes experience to ensure that whenever Mary is seen she looks just like the statue of her in the village church. That is why she is always so easy to recognize: that is how people know that it really is Mary whom they see.

In view of all this, it is not surprising that the word 'de-traditionalization' has come into use recently to describe the process by which communities undergoing modernization find themselves being progressively stripped of all their cultural traditions – all those beliefs, customs, experiences and so on which were once taken for granted as secure and inviolable.[2] They seemed so obviously right and intelligible, they stabilized communal life and they created the realities by which everyone lived: but now they have suddenly collapsed. People feel that they are in a moral void. They are shocked to find themselves quite unable to pass on their faith and values to the next generation.

An effect of de-traditionalization that needs to be noticed is that old beliefs suddenly lose meaning. Wittgenstein gives us a vivid illustration of this when he remarks in conversation that he just cannot imagine what sort of an event the creation of the world by God could possibly be. For thousands of years it had been perfectly clear to people that God made the world; or, if they denied the truth of that proposition, at least they seemed to have no problem about its meaning. But now Wittgenstein for the first time raises a doubt. Next time you hear someone say, 'Of course God made us, didn't he?', perhaps Wittgenstein's perplexity will suddenly fall upon you. You have snapshots of yourself as a baby, you know who your parents were, you know your mother bore you, you have your birth certificate, and you know a bit about human origins. So you know *exactly* how you were made. What on earth can it mean to say that it was after all *God* who made you? Why use a form of words that appears to deny what is biologically obvious?

For twenty-six centuries philosophers have been pointing out that tradition may require us to do and to believe some very odd things. The moment I just tried to evoke is the moment when we are suddenly wonderstruck. In that moment philosophy begins, and tradition has died.

Now virtually the entirety of religious belief and practice as we have received it comes to us from tradition. Tradition made it appear meaningful, tradition assured us it was all true, and tradition shaped the experiences that seemed to confirm its objective truth. But in the last generation or so there has been a sudden collapse of tradition. Local cultures have been engulfed by the enormously rapid growth of fully-globalized cultural activities and products, a growth still further accelerated in the early 1980s by the multiplication of communications satellites and the deregulation of financial markets. When products such as cars, cinema films, electronic goods and popular music are designed for a world market, it is clear that a world culture has arrived. By their choices, people show that they actually prefer the world-product to the local and traditional product.

Traditional culture, such as that of the Japanese, or the Orthodox Jew, or the Roman Catholic, can be and is preserved encapsulated in corners of society and corners of people's lives. But, when it is confined to these sealed-off corners, tradition is intellectually and morally without effect. It can be preserved for the tourist trade, and it may be regarded with nostalgia and admiration, but it no longer *does* anything. And because its symbolic vocabulary no longer engages with the lives people are actually living, it loses all meaning.

We have already noticed that Wittgenstein, although a strongly religious person, was in the 1930s finding himself simply unable to comprehend many of the most familiar propositions of traditional religious belief. Perhaps it was around that time that the collapse of tradition was beginning to take place. After all, Nietzsche, although extremely sensitive to language and very hostile to Christianity, never complains that he cannot understand religious beliefs: on the contrary, he regards Christianity as a complete and coherent system of thought. Wittgenstein may have been the first person, both of the highest talent and sympathetic to religious belief, to complain of sheer inability to understand some parts of it.

In the 1950s such complaints were much discussed; but unfortunately the debates about them were couched in a philo-

32

sophically mediocre language. The grumble was that theological
statements were not clearly meaningful, because nobody seemed
able to specify just what empirical difference it made whether
they were true or false. The scientific method had immense
prestige at that time. Its use to test the truth of theories seemed
a very powerful weapon against ignorance and superstition.
Here were traditionalists, claiming objective truth for their
religious and moral beliefs. So the critics said to them: 'Very
well. Are you willing to say how your beliefs might be tested?
Describe what would count as failure of the test, obliging you
to give the beliefs up.' And so on, with the critics saying that
if you hold that your religious and moral beliefs are objectively
true, but won't expose them to the risk of falsification, then you
are talking nonsense. The only claims that are worth taking
seriously are those that are testable; what's not testable is mean-
ingless and should be disregarded.

In this debate the philosophers (mostly) stuck to a crude
scientism, and the believers (mostly) accepted a crudely realistic
account of their own claims. So the philosophers (mostly)
won the argument, thus preparing the public for the next
generation's experience – the collapse of religious language.
Today the language of fundamentalism is ugly and empty
ranting, and the language of liberal religion is soothing but
empty waffle.

We can adopt neither vocabulary here – which is why this
study in post-Christian and post-traditional religious thought
has to take the form it does. When the tradition has finally
collapsed, no amount of repair-work can revive it. You must
reimagine and redevelop the whole site.

Accordingly, this book contains two little treatises, one on
metaphysics or general philosophy, and another (very short) one
on active and contemplative religion.

A treatise on metaphysics, because after the collapse of tradition we have to rethink everything if we are to find a style of
religious thinking that makes sense. And in any case, both in the
East and in the West the history of philosophy and the history
of religious thought were always intertwined. So it is that today

a transition from Philosophy to post-philosophy is taking place in parallel with the transition from 'organized' ecclesiastical Christianity to post-Christianity. Nobody has yet explained the affinity between the two transitions, and this now needs to be done.

In philosophy, we are talking about the change from old-style platonic realism to the new only-human philosophy that begins with William James and Nietzsche. The old realism was belief in an objective order of Reason, Reason out-there, a universal Reason that structured all the world, and which transcended all that was merely sensuous, merely human, and merely historical. But gradually during the nineteenth century eternal Reason came down to earth and became merely 'subjective', i.e. human and culturally-conditioned. The triumph of historical thinking and of Darwin completed the process. Now, we are on our own.

However, if there is no Reason out there, and if reason now is only-human, truth is only-human, knowledge is only-human and meaning itself is only-human, then it would seem that metaphysics is impossible. We are always stuck inside our own merely-human point of view, our own languages, and our own small stretch of historical time. If we don't participate in any objective and timeless universal Reason, we can never get to the standpoint for writing grand old-style metaphysics. It is dead, and cannot be resuscitated.

Philosophers have reacted to this new problem in various ways. Feuerbach and Nietzsche for example wrote philosophies of the future, from which there has developed a visionary and almost a science-fiction tradition. Wittgenstein, by contrast, gave up any attempt either to make large general statements or to build a system. Philosophy doesn't change anything, and cannot any longer pretend to deliver a special and privileged kind of knowledge. It should limit itself to small-scale jobs, tidying up, clarifying and re-ordering the ideas we presently have.

The difficulty with these strategies is that if we drop out of the World-View business, or if alternatively we encourage visionaries, we are leaving the field wide open to any number of ideologues, fundamentalists and crazies. Such people are a menace, and it has always been part of philosophy's task to combat them. We need now to reinvent metaphysics, at least in the very cautious sense of sketching the view of the world and the human condition that a reasonable person might currently hold. Somebody needs to try to say what it might be 'to see life steadily and to see it whole' today.

So I'm reinventing metaphysics (of a sort) and in doing so am struggling to keep a whole lot of different balls in the air at once. For example, the Arts people currently want to bring everything down to a motion of cultural Signs, and the Science people want to bring it all down to a purely mathematical Theory of Everything: the Universe as a slow-motion explosion, scattering radiation and tiny packets of energy. How do we combine these two approaches and, if we are always held within our own all-encompassing systems of representation, then whatever happened to the world and the self? Who paints all these pictures, and how do we know if they are pictures *of* something? In particular, I'm concerned about the status of our vast and gorgeous new scientific world-narrative. It describes in human words and mathematical symbols states of affairs alleged to have obtained billions of years before any language or mathematics existed. So let's take our new scientific narrative about the Universe, and subtract from it all the modern human language and the maths in which it is so anachronistically described. What is left?

Oops! Nothing is left. Nothing at all. So we have a philosophical problem.

3

How It Is

Until about 1690 or so, humanity's Other – that in relation to which it saw itself, understood itself and defined itself – was the supernatural world of gods, spirits, departed souls and the rest. It was very important to maintain proper relations with the other world, and this required the regular use of a special communication system. It was generally believed that the supernatural order had communicated to us the correct rituals and symbolic vocabulary that we needed to use, entrusting them to the priesthood. So it was that before the European Enlightenment most of humankind tended to see knowledge and truth and meaning, indeed the entire symbolic order and all the right ways of doing things, as having come down from above. Human beings hadn't themselves evolved their own languages and cultures and religions; rather, they were graciously permitted to participate in a prior, unchanging and greater Reality.

However, a cultural explosion had already begun in the fifteenth century, and by the end of the seventeenth century it was beyond doubt that the traditional cosmology was dead. Newton had demonstrated that unassisted human reason could construct a powerful system of mathematical physics. The final secularization of biology, psychology and social theory was not to be completed till the late nineteenth century, but today it is evident that humanity's Other is simply what we have recently come to call the environment.

It now appears, then, that we human beings are alone. We evolved our own languages and cultures. It was after all just we ourselves who developed the entire realm of knowledge and truth and meaning, indeed the entire symbolic order and all the right ways of doing things. It follows that religion's traditional self-understanding was mistaken. We made religion, and it is central to culture; but it is not quite what it has hitherto supposed itself to be.

These considerations have helped to shift attention from the supernatural world to the religious system. It is highly typical of the modern period that religion in many quarters comes to be valued, and perhaps even practised, chiefly for cultural and nationalistic or ethnic reasons. The effective religious object has become not God but Jewishness, not Christ but Anglicanism, not Siva but Hindu nationalism, not God but Islam and pan-Arabism, not God but faith in God, not God but the church, and not even primarily the church, but 'Roman Catholicism'. In a way, the religious system stands in front of and displaces the old religious object – a shift, as we shall see, that is not without its dangers.

First, though, we must consider the possibility that the change we are describing may have begun a very long time ago. Before the birth of Christ, it is reported that the Maccabees 'were bravely and honourably fighting on behalf of *Iudaismos*' (II Maccabees 2.21, cf. 8.1; 14.38). Not God, but Judaism or Jewishness. Wilfred Cantwell Smith comments: 'This is perhaps the first time in human history that a religion has a name.'[1] At one time God had a name – indeed, every god had a proper name – but there was no proper name for religion. Indeed, you were not particularly aware of your religion as a coherent and distinctive cultural system. Think of early Greece: its gods remain lively personalities, but its 'religion' is almost forgotten. The god was so patent and vivid that you scarcely had time to think about the ritual vocabulary in which you were communicating with him or her. But the centuries passed, oracles and prophecies ceased, God fell silent and became distant and impersonal, and the practice of one's religion replaced the old immediacy. A certain fetichization of the religious system began: because it was now seen as being distinctive and had its own identity, it got a proper name of its own and began to be perceived as having the power to give you your identity. You identify yourself as an adherent with others of a particular named religious system. Thus the gods are lost, and we are well on the way to the horrors of today's fundamentalism and ethnic obsessions.

That's why we are post-Christian. At the beginning of the tradition people could feel free and uninhibited; they lived in the open air with their gods. The God spoke to you, addressing you by name. But in the end the fetichized and self-obsessed religious system, the Ism, eclipses the old religious object and becomes itself the ultimate idol. It quenches the spirit entirely, and religion becomes unendurably oppressive and claustrophobic.

Do you see the implications of this? It implies that the Age of the Church, the age of the objectified religious system, was always likely to be rather short. The old, overwhelmingly powerful and immediate God of the prophets had already faded long before the rise of what was eventually to be called 'Christianity'. Jesus may be seen as attacking a process of traditionalization, codification and objectification, which was well under way in his own time. It prevailed in Jewry, and it prevailed amongst Christians too. The Kingdom-style of life that Jesus taught was meant to be a fresh-air alternative to life within an oppressive religious system. But his own message was lost: the New Testament is the book of the eclipse of Jesus by Christianity. Long afterwards, in about 1690, the argument between the Ancients and the Moderns was resolved in favour of the Moderns. Tradition and ecclesiastical faith began to lose their former authority. From Spinoza and the Deists onwards, there develops a strong desire for a freer and more Enlightened form of religious life, a desire that has grown ever-stronger as the old religious systems have grown more and more irrational and authoritarian.

So we need to escape: and it is especially important to escape from today's worsening religious tribalism and enthnocentrism. We need to claim religious freedom in our new only-human world. So what follows is going to be metaphysics, or rather post-metaphysics, and it's going to seem austere, no doubt, because there is so much rubbish that has to be thrown out. I'm still chasing my insane fifteen-year ambition – to write the first not-untruthful Western religious book. The first ever, though there are certainly some not-untruthful Eastern books.

A friend objects to the hubris of the last two sentences, so I should explain: Heidegger, in his meditation on the history of philosophy, says that we in the West were not content to let Being be. We wanted to think it – as the One, as the realm of Ideas, as the Logos, as the world-ground; and in due course as First Cause and predestinating sovereign Will. The theme is that the idea of God, especially, brings Being too far forward into objectification. Eventually, it turns into absolute Power.

So it was that Western religious thought came to see life's chief End as being to get as close as one can to a single supreme concentration of pure Spiritual Power. Worship it, commit yourself to it, and become its servant, working to extend its sway over other people's lives, too. Western religious writing accordingly became a persuasive, seductive or threatening rhetoric deployed in the service of such Power – so much so that even today people cannot recognize a text as religious, unless it has the character of seeking to manipulate the reader in the service of spiritual power. *There* lies the 'untruth' I speak of.

In a strange way, people even expect religious writing to be an attempt at deception – as is indicated by their indignant reaction to the rare phenomenon of an honest Bishop. 'It is utterly dishonest of him to be so honest', they complain. 'Why can't he be dishonest, as an honest Bishop should?' Exactly. So my hyperbole expresses my sense that I am flailing about in a trap that is hard to escape. It is very difficult to find a style that is both religious and truthful.

Truth, *truth*? – who wants truth? In American popular cinema everything is real: extra-terrestrials, mermaids, time-travel, body-swaps, gods, witches, poltergeists, the souls of dead people, Bigfoot, talking animals, monsters – anything you fancy may and does come bursting into your average suburban family's life. In children's literature, in church, and in the cinema we show how nostalgic we still are for the old thickly-populated universe of tradition, with all its invisible beings and magical powers. We still wriggle and wriggle as we try to defer accepting what in our hearts we all know to be the truth: humanity's

Other is now just the world described by the natural sciences, the Environment. We have no personal or quasi-personal Other. Language is so completely human, so minutely adapted to our way of life and our practical needs, that anything that uses our language has just got to be human. Our language is as specific to us as our human bodies are.

I am not saying anything novel. I am only reminding you of what you already know. The human world now stands alone. It is the world of language. That is, it is the world of natural language plus all its various specialized extensions and offshoots such as the vocabularies of mathematics, ballet, roadsigns, music and so on. All our thinking is transacted in linguistic and other signs, so that our world is for us always already encoded in the flux of our signs. Even raw sense-experience requires general concepts (i.e., signs) for us to be able to get hold of it, and for it to become our conscious experience. Thus both the supposed inner world of the mind, and the supposed 'outer' world of physical cosmology, are always already laid over with language, and coded into the flux of language. Our language has an outer face, the world, and an inner face, subjectivity or 'experience', and we have no extra-linguistic access either to the world or to ourselves.

Professor Stephen Hawking, in *A Brief History of Time*, has some animadversions upon the prominence of language in modern philosophy, as if he thinks that the Universe of cosmology is surely quite obviously a much bigger object than language. What a pity that he could not find some medium other than language in which to make his point! But the fact is that the doing of physics and mathematics is a manipulation of human signs, and the Universe can only ever present itself already encoded in the movement of a human language. Scientists are not philosophers, and they may tend to suppose that language is something that goes on only in one small corner of the universe. They may think that when we move out to contemplate the formation of galaxies and the birth and death of stars, we are moving outside language. The error arises because when we are trained in science we are trained systematically to bracket out our own subjectivity and pay no attention to it. As a result, scientists tend to overlook their own linguisticality and the effect that it has upon the status of their work. It is easy to forget that one is always still within language even as one fancies oneself to be thinking about something supposedly outside it. We innocently imagine that thinking-about is referential and takes us outside language, whereas thinking-about is a motion of signs, representation, which remains firmly inside language. Even ostension is still a linguistic operation. A man who supposes he has moved outside language is like a man who searches for his spectacles, forgetting that he wouldn't be able to search unless they were already on his nose. All his supposing happens inside language – which means that the Big Bang, and the Universe itself, are conjured up only by language and can appear to us only within language.

Thus our language and our whole world are coextensive. Each stretches just as far as the other, making the world of language radically outsideless. There is no non-human language, no non-human knowledge, and no non-human vision of the world against which we can check our own perspectives. We cannot any longer look for timeless and objective standards of meaning, independent of the flux of current human usage. There is no objective Truth of things independent of the current human consensus. The objective world, and all meaning, truth and value, are thus now radically humanized. Everything is given to us, and we can say of things only that they are what they are for us. Nothing and nobody independent of ourselves has, or indeed could have, the answers.

The new philosophical state of affairs that I am describing has been around for well over a century, being anticipated in Feuerbach and Marx, and then clearly expressed both in James's and Schiller's 'humanism' and Nietzsche's 'anti-realism'. Its most rigorous and lucid statement so far is probably Wittgenstein's. But we need to push the argument rather further than has been done before, in order to open up the new religious situation.

*　　*　　*

What can we be sure of? What is there that may serve as a starting-point for philosophy? There is language, because here we are already immersed in it and we could scarcely *not* be in it. There is no way of self-consistently denying the existence of language. And there are also two possibility-conditions of language which must already have been fulfilled. One is temporality, an ordered linear succession of events: it is needed because for there to be language, signs must be arranged in a linear order and scanned successively. And the second condition is materiality, because language requires some sort of body or material vehicle.

What is materiality? We need a sufficiently powerful metaphor to link together the way the world is objectively with the way we ourselves produce and experience language subjectively, the point being that the objective world is produced on the 'outer' face of language, and the subjective realm – the world of feeling – on its 'inner' face. There must be what theologians call a 'double homoöusios', in that the stuff language is made of must be 'of one substance' with what the world is made of, and also of one substance with what our subjectivity is made of.

Now, our physical theory represents the Universe as an immense explosion, a vast discharge of energy; and it reduces matter to swarms of minute packets of energy, ripples or wavelets, tiny moving twists or kinks in the fabric of space-time. At the same time, on the subjective side, we have long reduced our sense-experience to a stream of minute impingements that cause vibrations to move upon the sensitive surfaces of the body. In addition, the production of language itself clearly calls for a certain expenditure of energy. Language is always expressive, its motion involving a certain discharge of *e*motion.

So we seek a metaphor that will connect that vast outpouring discharge of energies in which the physical world consists, and also the outpouring discharge of psychic energies or feelings in which our life consists, with the motion of language in time.

Remember, I am again insisting that the three worlds – the objective world, the world of language, and the subjective world of our feelings and valuations – have to be, they really do have to be, precisely co-extensive. None of them does, *or can possibly*, outrun the others. The number and nicety of the distinctions that can be made in our language correlates precisely with the complexity of the objective world that we can know, and it must also correlate precisely with the fineness of our feelings and the evaluative discriminations that we can make. The world, the Word and the self are a coequal Trinity. One continuous outpouring of language-formed energies is on its outer face objective reality and on its inner face the subjective world of our thoughts and feelings. Notice too a further beautiful analogy between the microcosm and the macrocosm: like the Universe in our current physical theory, a human being is a coiled spring that releases most of its locked-up energies near the beginning of its life, and subsequently unwinds and dissipates its remaining energies more and more slowly. Haven't you noticed the prodigious emotional force of babies? But, like the Universe, we cool down as our energies gradually pour out, scatter, and disperse into nothingness. There is no consummation, only dissipation: life isn't going anywhere, it's just going everywhere. Notice (and file away the point until later) that on this account life and death are the same thing. They coincide: the outpouring and scattering of energies in which the world's life consists, and our life consists, is also our death and the heat-death of the universe. The Second Law of Thermodynamics makes living and dying two ways of describing the same process. Burning, we burn out. But if these considerations seem pessimistic, let us not fail to note that, both in the Universe's case and in our own, it is only after the initial extremely high energy-levels are dissipated that the most valuable and complex objects can be produced. The Universe has to cool down a great deal before it can give birth to living things, or human brains; and we have to cool down a great deal before we can ourselves produce our best work.

So much, then, for the need to harmonize and unify under a single metaphor the subjective world of our own outpouring feelings and valuations, the world of language, and the objective world of nature. What has been said implies that the world of perception, the world of sense-experience, is not and cannot be any wider than the world of the common language. Many will dispute this point, so before I proceed I'm going to try to secure it.

Three hundred years ago John Locke – following a long tradition – denied that we have any innate ideas, and declared that prior to experience the human mind is a blank slate.[2] Most people connect the phrase with the image of the mind as a screen or a mirror that produces a reflection or copy of external reality. They see thoughts as mental pictures of things, and will be startled by my suggestion that we need to give a linguistic account even of perception.

Locke's choice of the word slate (*tabula*) is, however, significant. A slate is something for writing on. Could an incoming sense-experience perhaps light up, not just a blank area of the slate, but a word already written on it? So let us try updating Locke's image by comparing the mind instead with a Japanese typewriter.

The *tabula* on top of a Japanese typewriter is a flat metal frame or grid in which are embedded up to ten thousand characters, 100 x 100, with the typeface on each square metal peg pointing downwards. The board is moved into place; it *experiences* a punch, and the appropriate character is printed out upon the page below.

Similarly, I am suggesting that we may picture our sensibility as being very highly pre-programmed with language. Our mothers' gift to us, the mother-tongue. A sense-experience is an impact upon a sensory surface which activates one or more words. Culture has programmed us with language in such a way that perception is recognition, and recognizing something is having a word for it.

This account may seem baffling, but it does avoid one difficulty of the mirror or screen theory of perception, namely its liability to run into an infinite regress when we ask ourselves, 'Who looks in the mirror? Who sees what is happening on the screen?' Many people picture our visual cortex as resembling a television receiver. Like a television aerial – and, especially, like a satellite dish – the eye picks up very delicate electromagnetic vibrations which the visual cortex processes, to convert them into a picture. Then the question arises of who looks at the picture. Does the inner observer of the mental picture need himself to form a picture of the picture, and so on?

There is a still more serious problem, too. In the case of television two distinct processes take place, one of encoding and one of decoding. In the studio the camera and the transmitting equipment encode the picture we are to view and broadcast it through the ether. In the home the receiver picks up and decodes the signal and presents us with an exact re-creation of what the cameraman sees through his viewfinder. We don't doubt that the decoding process exactly reverses the encoding process. There is a *pre-planned* one-to-one correspondence between the two processes. The receiver has been expressly designed to undo the work of the transmitter. But in the case of the human eye and the visual cortex, we cannot similarly claim that the decoding operation reverses step-by-step a previous operation of encoding. Where's the alleged encoding going on? There is none; and the visual cortex does not decode. It builds.

Surely, when I look now at my desk I see, not a picture or a reproduction of my desk, but just my desk? I can tell you what I see, and I can show it to you, so that you can see it too. We see one thing, the same thing – and don't we all in practice equate perceiving or experiencing with the capacity to describe or bear witness? That is why I'm trying to vary the metaphor, from the television receiver to the Japanese typewriter.

Since classical times the vocabulary in which perception is discussed has been mainly passive. One is still, one watches, one takes in. The whole vocabulary of contemplation, theory, vision, observation and so on suggests reflective motionlessness. So let us instead emphasize that our senses evolved to serve the practical needs of a living organism. We are complicated quivering bundles of energies. We strive to maintain and to reproduce ourselves. Goings-on in our environment *impinge* upon us, and may or may not be *relevant* to our survival.

They have to be *assessed*, they have to be *evaluated* as being potentially threatening or promising, they have to be *interpreted*, and we must *respond* by behaving appropriately.

If we happen to be social animals, the appropriate behavioural response will often be to signal very promptly to other members of our group. Biologically, it makes sense that perception should instantly activate exclamation. More generally, it makes biological sense that our perceptual systems should be very closely tied in with our communication codes, and the more highly social an animal gets to be the more intimate the association we should expect to find between sensation and speech.

For the most communicative animal of all, which is ourselves, there is no point in our having any ineffable private experiences that can mean nothing to anyone else. Indeed, it's not clear how such experiences could possibly mean anything to us either. For us, the most sociable creatures, it makes sense that everything experienced should go straight into our forms of expression and description. We need to put it into words, right away – and therefore we need to be equipped with words to put it into.

And that is why I say that for us human beings a perception is the activation of a meaning, and that the world presents itself as a flux of language-formed events. Animals respond to sensory stimuli, but nobody can have conscious experience unless some kind of language or sign-system has turned her sensations into perceptions. Language structures experience precisely in order to make it into conscious experience of a common world.

Now comes the difficult bit, the bit that tips us into antirealism. If you accept this argument, carrying it through and applying its conclusion also to itself, then you grasp that we are always inside language. We have no entirely pre-linguistic experience or access to reality, a realization which reaches back and makes merely metaphorical the earlier stages of the present argument. We now see that we were using language to conjure up a 'picture' of how things might be out there prior to language.

Such a picture may – as I shall later try to indicate – be

developed by a transcendental argument. Language needs time to unfold, and it also needs a 'body' to ride upon, a body made of discharging energies like the signal from a radio transmitter. Language presupposes a world of scattering energies, of systems striving to maintain themselves, of conflicts, interactions and communications between systems, and so on. On this basis we may try to construct a transcendental framework, clothe it with metaphors, and so build up a world-picture. Soon we are liable to find ourselves talking as if we think there is a real world, out there and independent of language, which duplicates the-world-in-language.

Duplicates: an antirealist is a person who objects strongly to the redundancy of that duplication. We don't need two worlds. The one we have got is fine. The common world constructed by people who share a common language is enough. The most comfortable account is the one that brings everything down to one level, a languagey continuum in which we are ourselves immersed. Everything is what it seems to be; that is, what the common language says it is. So the antirealist argument circles round, rather as George Berkeley's argument circles round, to bring everything back to common sense.[1] I don't wish to deny anything obvious; only to dispense with some unnecessary and misleading ways of speaking.

A happy consequence of all this is that we just don't need to make the customary mind/matter distinction. The supposedly inward and spiritual world of mind and thought and the supposedly outer and physical world of material bodies are not different in kind. They are made out of the same stuff, they are continuous with each other, and they overlap extensively. Indeed there is no very clear frontier between them at all.

Jacques Lacan pointed out long ago that because the mirror-image of the human body seems to us when we first encounter it to have such a clear outline, we are inclined all our lives to fancy that the self is a much more clear-cut and distinct entity than it is. In fact, its boundaries are blurred and constantly shifting, with material crossing back and forth over them all the time.

Come here for a moment. I'm sitting at my desk on one of those knee-stools that claims to keep your back straight. Trying to pull some sentences into shape, because I want to finish this section, which was running through my head all last night. A slight ache inside-top of the eyeballs – I hate having to wear spectacles. A bus buzzing in the street, the chatter of tourists, sunshine. I've been working two hours, getting thirsty – well, hungry actually. Turning my head I see people setting lunch out in the Hall across the court, and indeed it *is* about 12.30 p.m., with the shadows short and hard. Why not?

... Where was I? I was in the stream of language-formed events, which encompasses and flows through both the 'outer' realm and the 'inner'. Indeed, in the everyday business of life we are, most of the time, unaware of any very clear distinction between them. Roughly, we seem ready to assign phrases and clauses which include first-person pronouns, and refer to feelings, desires and intentions, to the 'inner' world of the self, and the rest we would assign to the outer, public world. The statements assigned to the public world have the property of making up a sort of *mosaic*. They stand in prepositional relations to each other: side by side, before and after, cause and effect. Assemble and systematize them, and they'll fit together to comprise an articulated space-time world of bodies within which I'm a subject with a point of view, with feelings and interests. The reason why the line between the self and the world is blurred is that my feelings as-it-were reach out, to influence what features of the external world it is that get picked out for attention and report. For example, an hour ago I was evidently alert for signs that it was lunchtime. My body said lunchtime, and my visual field found something that replied, 'Lunch!' – and now there is a knock on the door and in comes my daughter, looking purposeful because she has Plans for me.

... Where was I, again? I construct myself out of first-person sentences that refer to purposes, feelings and intentions, and I construct others out of second and third-person sentences which ascribe intentions, feelings and desires to them. But I don't at any point feel any great need to draw a sharp distinction between the inner world and inner space of the mind, and the outer world and geometrical space of physical bodies. Both worlds are made of the same stuff, namely language, which runs equally easily and without interruption through both of them. Nothing blocks its flow, and I don't see how there could be anything that *did* block it.

So I recommend that we see the world as consisting simply in the one continuous stream of language-formed events. Like a novel, indeed. That is how it presents itself, that is what there seems to be, and that is sufficient. So that is what there is.

The world presents itself as a continuous stream of language-formed events. Through these events energy is continuously being discharged, borne away on waves or spreading ripples.

Unlike the atoms and the sense-data of some other systems of thought, the energy-events that we postulate are not atomic or independent of each other. On the contrary, the world is very dense, like the surface of a pond in a hailstorm, with vast numbers of ripples, splatters and wavelets tangled up with each other, superimposed upon each other, criss-crossing each other.

Thus what is given is not a heap of marbles, but a dense texture. And in its reception by us it is already language-formed in more than one respect. Culture has so programmed us with language that any event, to be apprehended at all, must be read as the activation of a sign, and the relations between events must present themselves as being already language-formed. That is, between different energy-events there are already language-like relations – relationships conjunctive, prepositional, adjectival, adverbial and so forth. So the world is apprehended by being read: but its texture is so dense that the same world-events may enter in different ways, and quite independently of each other, into a variety of different readings.

Look about you now, at what's in your visual field and within earshot. You are the subjective aspect of the stream of events before you. You are not a blank slate: on the contrary, you are such a highly linguistic being that the bare occurrence of the event, the vibe traversing your sensibility, is already a motion of language. That is how the so-called 'mind' works: percept is always already formed by concept, and the world-event, the fleeting ripple, is always already a language-event. Looking is already seeing: you see the book in your hand, the cat on the carpet. You see, indeed, not just facts but phrases. You think in words and you perceive through words: more than that, you perceive under the forms of a physical-object language. Just as you look, everything drops into place. Beautiful: the world as text. But the world is so dense, and there are so many vocabularies, that it can be and is read in many other different ways. To return to the metaphor of the pond in the hailstorm, so many things are happening at once on the pond's surface that there isn't any single privileged, exactly-right, description of what's happening. The world, like your brain, is a seething cauldron of language. It is like the interior of an urban public house during the evening, with large numbers of voices chattering away in several languages, and with in addition several lines of music and background noise from buses, dogs and whatnot. It all seems at first to be an incomprehensible babble, but with an effort you can single out one line of intelligible stuff to follow. Cock an ear, and you might be able to switch to the music, or to the talk at the next table. You cannot take in everything, but you are able to pick out a few different strands, and to switch your concentration from one of them to another.

Three main ways of reading the world need to be distinguished. In so far as the stream of world-events is read and interpreted mathematically, it becomes the world of theoretical physics. In so far as the stream of events presents and is read in our physical-object language, it becomes the everyday life-world. And in so far as the stream of events is read in and through an aesthetic vocabulary of feelings, valuations, preferences, intentions and so forth, it becomes the world of subjectivity.

Thus the metaphysical doctrine I propose is that there is only one (immensely tangled and dense) flow of events. But it is always overlaid and formed by language; that is, it is always *read* in one way or another. Thus our linguisticality simultaneously gives to us consciousness, and to the world structure.

50

Each way of reading the world is a way of world-making, just as in quantum physics the world only becomes fully determinate in our observation of it. Inevitably, the doing of a subject helps to produce its subject-matter. We don't first see the world and then construct theories about it: rather, in developing our theories we are learning how best to form our world. And indeed world-visions may be more or less objective in aim. Read and understood mathematically, the world becomes the world of theoretical physics, perhaps the most nearly-objective vision of the world that can be produced. (However, notice that mathematics too is only human. We invented all its signs and all the rules for manipulating them. Mathematics is just another language, a way of reading aspects of the world. And to what is applied mathematics applied? We can produce only words – energies, waves, velocities.) At the opposite extreme from physics, a painter's feeling-response to colour represents one of the most expressly subjective visions of the world that can be developed. Somewhere in between the two, the vocabulary of modern biology is of outstanding interest. For biology reads the world in terms of life's interest in itself as it conducts its own astonishingly-varied local rearguard action against the general movement of all things into nothingness, whilst at the same time each individual living thing strives with all its might to pass life on, and in doing so to die. Thus what is moving and beautiful about modern biology's way of reading life is that each living thing – including you and me, of course – both participates in the general slipping-away of all things into nothingness *and* conducts its little local rearguard action by converting its own drive to death into the drive to pass on its genes to the next generation. It is as if every living thing knows how we should live. Everything slips away, everything participates in the general movement towards ever-greater entropy. But life itself has the trick of converting its own passing away into a continual joyous renewal of itself (a point very well made, incidentally, at the end of the opera *The Cunning Little Vixen*).

Clichés inherited from antiquity lead us to think of doing philosophy, and of the practice of Buddhist meditation, as ways of preparing for death. They teach us, perhaps, stillness, detachment, emptiness – the idea being that the more relaxed, calm and emptied-out we become the more blissful we feel. Even the capillary vessels relax, and warmth steals over us. The moment of death may thus be viewed as a state of total relaxation, and therefore of final and snuffed-out impersonal bliss, as the afflicted individual consciousness ceases. That is something to look forward to, and maybe it is the biological truth of contemplative religion. But there is also a less-often-noticed biological truth of active religion. In sex and in giving birth we pump away, recklessly pouring out our life in order to give life, and we embrace *le petit mort* enthusiastically in a climax in which the affirmation of life, the acceptance of death, and the giving of life are united.[4]

Recall, while we are with this metaphor, that the self exactly and completely coincides with the flux in which it is inscribed. In the act of sex, and in giving birth, we seem to have no wish to pretend that we are anything other than what we are. We don't in any way attempt to distance ourselves inwardly from the flux of signs and feelings and events. On the contrary, we plunge into it and pour ourselves out as if unto death.

Contrast another case, that of the visual field. We have a curiously persistent wish to postulate an observer of the visual field, a pure ego, something that is never itself seen but is always presupposed, tucked way on the inward side of the visual field. However, there is no such transcendental observer; for if there needs to be an observer in your head looking at your visual field, how could he see it? He'd need to have a picture in *his* head, and so on *ad infinitum*. So the visual field has no observer. Its seenness is the seeing of it. The visual field itself shows not merely what is seen, but what seeing is. Within my visual field elements of the world are so related to each other as to become my seeing of them. The visual field is synthesized, bright, conscious and spatio-temporally ordered. A chunk of the world is constructed *as seen*. Just by being what it is the visual field is seen; and no additional observer of it is required. Do you see the admirable truth here? The more completely we can give up the illusions of transcendence, the more completely we are content to be nothing but a set of relations amongst elements of the flux of language-formed events, the more completely the world is given to us as *ours*.[5] The brightness of the visual field is identical with the consciousness of our conscious experience and *is* the world's coming to life and taking on beauty and interest in and through our feeling of it. In a popular idiom, ordinary people seem to make a contrast between what's really out there and what's only 'in your mind' ; but I am trying to undo that very contrast. It is the fact that it is 'in your mind' that puts it 'out there'. Consciousness and the mind are out in front, interwoven with the world, visible in and as its present brightness and order.

I have been trying, through various metaphors, to present a vision of the world appropriate for post-darwinian human beings. Our spirituality will seek to be true to life, in that it will be not thrifty but prodigal. Life recklessly expends itself and thereby renews itself. And in its own violent and extravagant self-expenditure, life teaches us that the more completely we accept the message of radical immanence and give ourselves over to the flux of things, the more the world gives itself to us.

(Try it *now*, with your own visual field. You are just the co-present seenness of what's before you. You are out there in it, in much the way that Paul Cézanne is in one of his own still-life paintings. And the point here can be made in linguistic terms, for the words we'd want to use in spelling out what's in the painting overlap a lot with words we'd want to use in talking about Paul Cézanne the person. The words the painting is made of overlap a lot with the words Cézanne is made of; so he really *did* put a lot of himself into his work. He *really* did.)

We have now two further features of the way the world presents itself to be considered. It is edgeless, unbounded or outsideless; and although it is temporal and time is unidirectional, there is also a sense in which the world is sempiternal.

The world, I said, presents itself as a single, very dense and continuous stream of language-formed events. But language is in several respects immeasurable and endless. Because every natural language is a system of differences, each word in a one-language dictionary is defined in terms of others – its neighbours, antonyms, synonyms, uses – and so on for ever. The whole system has no single point of entry and no exit: rather, one thing leads to another, and so on. The world of words is endless much as interpretation is endless, and as wandering thought is endless.

In addition, the strange semantic space in which the great contrasts and oppositions are inscribed is measureless, and strangely hard to think. We may begin like Genesis, with the various cosmic boundaries and horizons. Easy enough: with a single sweeping gesture the cosmic line is drawn. But if we next try to imagine the length of the line between the possible and the impossible, the space bisected by that line, and what there is on either side of it, we boggle. When, in addition, we try to superimpose upon that a consideration of the many spaces also opened up by the other great metaphysical oppositions, we find ourselves lost in a hall of mirrors with infinite vistas opening up in all directions.

Thirdly, language is also endless in the sense that in any natural language an immeasurably-large number of grammatically well-formed sentences can be constructed, each sentence being in principle usable on a variety of distinct occasions, in a variety of different language-games, and being then taken up in many different ways to be subjected to a variety of different interpretations.

Thus, in various respects language is immeasurable and endless. But the world and language and the self are, as we said earlier, co-extensive, the objective world being (as one might say) language's 'outer' face, and subjectivity or selfhood being language's 'inner' face. The very same motion of language makes the world bright, and us conscious. So the world and the self are also immeasurable and endless, as language is. Nor is this suggestion either novel or surprising. C.S. Peirce, in 1868, is already to be found teaching the endlessness of the motion of thought-signs. Freud finds that the process of psychoanalysis has no clearly-marked beginning or ending. Einstein and his successors in physical cosmology develop, gradually more completely, a representation of the cosmos as finite but unbounded. J. M. E. McTaggart, unusual amongst the philosophers, equates immortality with the purely immanent endlessness of a loving reciprocal knowledge and communion between persons. Thus the endlessness of the world, of language, and of subjectivity is not a novel idea. But I have recalled it in order to revise a traditional metaphysical contrast, that between what is within and what is beyond the limits of thought.

Since very early times human beings have drawn a distinction between things near-at-hand, familiar, accessible and easily-understood, and other things which are beyond our reach because they are mysterious, transcendent and perhaps forbidden to mere mortals like us. It was thought that the Universe is like a great house, in which we live below stairs. Our own realm is completely familiar to us, but the sacred realm above is a different matter. Our access to it is strictly limited, and we never fully understand the life that goes on there. Those above let us know only what they consider it needful that we should know in order that we may serve them well. To seek to know more 'would not be our place'. Thus a sense of cosmic etiquette – not to mention common prudence – decrees that we humans ought reverently to acknowledge what people call 'a dimension of mystery' in the world and in our lives. Mystery equals 'upstairs'.

We must now reject that entire way of thinking. On our radically-immanent account, the world is all on one level. There is nothing off the page, nothing between the lines, and nothing behind the scenes. There is only the flux of language-formed events, the dance of appearances. What appears is what there is. There's nothing else, nothing forbidden and nothing 'mysterious'. It's all as perspicuous as these sentences. In its flux, the world gives itself as completely to you as you are given into it.

However, whereas Spinoza demonstrated his metaphysics *ordine geometrico*, and so aimed to produce a system of the world as tightly interconnected as a Buckminster-Fuller geodesic dome, our metaphysics is literary. It is literary because it is written in prose and admits it, whereas Spinoza's didn't. This text, this chain of signs, is a simplified image of what the world is. The movement of signs is not deterministic, but is governed by literary requirements. We are looking for associations, inter-pretations and powerful unifying metaphors, aiming as we go for a text that will be reflexively true to itself and to its own message as it recommends a life-view and a life-policy.

For an objective world and a subjective realm both made now of language only, we offer a metaphysics demonstrated *more poetica*. So in place of the old mysterious transcendent order, we will acknowledge that the movement of signs is never strictly predictable. Language and interpretation being endless, there is and always will be scope for surprise, for innovation and for theatrical *coups* of one kind and another. We don't believe in mysteries, we don't believe in progress and we don't believe in any future totalization of the world, but we do believe in art, and in the creative religious imagination.

We also find a certain sense in which the world is now timeless. This is happening because two different conceptions of linear time, once very powerful, are now in difficulties. Newton's absolute Time, linear, continuous and mathematical, has been relativized by recent developments in physics; and more recently still there has been a loss of belief in the classic Western notion of History as progressively advancing towards a future universal consummation. Nietzsche already says that if we cannot bank on the occurrence of some future event to make our lives hitherto worthwhile, then we are going to have to find and affirm the meaning and the whole worth of life here, now and in the present moment. We can no longer postdate the cheques. There is Nothing to look forward to.

This suggests that in the postmodern world that comes after the end of History we'll need to affirm the *Now* of the lilies of the field and the birds of the air, the *Now* of art, the *Now* of Dōgen's Soto Zen Buddhism, and the *Now* of Jesus and the Sermon on the Mount. Affirming this *Now* might usefully be coupled with an attempt to get into a steady and sustainable relationship with the natural environment.

All very well, and all very familiar. But everything we have recently come to understand about language appears at first sight to contradict it. Language is radically temporal, and it seems to preclude the possibility of any eternal Presence of the fullness of being and meaning. Language *is* transience. It slips by, at such a rate that the object of our desire never fully arrives, and before it has come is already disappearing. We can't affirm an eternal Now, if the Now never quite gets here.

A constant falling-away into loss and dissolution, then: but also a constant renewal. The image of a fountain has been awaiting us, because in speaking of the world as a flux of language-formed events we called up a picture of a constantly-maintained uprush of energies that arch upwards, spread, scatter and are borne away and lost. The image combines the unidirectional rush of everything into oblivion with a certain stillness, a fountain in a garden being a traditional topic of meditation and symbol of life.

The image also suggests how there might be a world in which time's arrow indeed always keeps pointing in the same direction, but in which there is no general long-term Goal towards which all events are orchestrated. The fountain flows in the same direction all the time, but it's not going anywhere. And indeed these considerations help to bring out the reason why our modern sense of time and timescales has become so disturbed. With the development of high-speed mechanical transport and communications since the early nineteenth century we have globalized a Newtonian sort of clock-time, universal, mathematical, linear and continuous, the time of time-tables, which in turn is keyed into a now-globalized historical time and astronomical time. It seems as if a single vast linear time-scale now hangs over and controls everything; *but*, strangely, the very same railway trains, airplanes and so on that have standardized time have also been relativizing it, giving us a sharper appreciation of the way distance, velocity and time-scale are interrelated. The effects are noticed not just in physics, but in everyday experience. Seen at long-distance the airplane drifts only slowly across the sky, the column of vehicles rushing along a motorway looks like a tailback, and the cascade tumbling down a hillside becomes a shiny motionless snail-track. Conversely, under the microscope we find a bustle of activity in a drop of pondwater and even within a single cell.

But the most extreme case of the relativity of the speed of time is the night sky, the traditional symbol of changeless perfection. What only a century ago were called 'the fixed stars' are now colossal nuclear furnaces consuming themselves and developing black holes in their hearts, whilst also exploding apart from each other at high speed. So the stars are now emblems at once of eternity and of the extremest violence and instability imaginable; and the same cultural developments that have led to the setting-up of the first fully-globalized dating system and time-scale have also had the effect of relativizing all our time-scales – making us aware, perhaps, of how much the pace of life can vary from one place to another.

Hence the fountain, a complex and interesting symbol of life's insubstantiality, its rush into oblivion and its ceaseless self-renewal. A symbol too of healing and refreshment, associated with the oasis and the pleasure garden. The notion of an activity so effortless and evenly-sustained that it coincides with a profound stillness is often found in Western metaphysics after Aristotle[6] as a symbol of God; but the fountain is perhaps better seen in Mahayana Buddhist terms. It is utterly Empty and fleeting, yet blissful to contemplate. It moves so fast it's still: it's so transient it's eternal. And there's a faint reminder of a point in physical theory. Fountains sometimes recycle their own water, and in physics there is a suggestion that nature's most energetic processes create as by-products tachyons, particles which travel faster than light and so go racing back in time to fuel the Big Bang. Along some such lines physical theory may be able to develop a picture of the world as cyclical: in its passing-away it continually gives birth to itself, self-subsistent in its very insubstantiality. Dying, it refuels its own birth.

Thoroughgoing naturalism in Western thought so far has

usually ended by claiming that atoms or the world-as-a-whole are necessary beings. But I am now talking about something of which the West has hitherto known nothing: a world that flits away so fast all the time that it keeps on bringing itself back again. Usually in the West it has been claimed that the contingent cannot stand alone, but needs to be grounded in or supported by the necessary – a line of argument which has often ended by making everything either mechanistically or rationally necessary. But the vision of the world as a dance of scattering featherlight energies-read-as-signs moves in the opposite direction. It doesn't explain the contingent by deriving it somehow from the necessary, but instead radicalizes contingency until it becomes self-sustaining and no longer needs any ulterior grounding or aim.

The image of the world as a fountain recalls other images of the world as endlessly, cyclically self-renewing: Siva's ring of fire, the serpent with its tail in its mouth, and the circles of Dante's cosmology that undergo inversion at the summit of Paradise and regroup around the mystic Rose. There are philosophical circles, too: Spinoza's rationalist metaphysics, Nietzsche's eternal return of the same.

Imagine representing a four-dimensional spacetime world as like a torus, a vast doughnut shape with a narrow central hole. The motion of all things starts at the smallest circle, around the central hole, and spreads out, up and over to the point of the Universe's greatest expansion around the outer circumference of the torus. Then it comes round underneath and back to its starting-point, so that the 'initial singularity' is also a black hole. The End becomes also the Beginning. Then forget the starting-point and imagine the streaming motion as continuous, without beginning or end, in such a way that the entire doughnut is made of nothing else but its own ceaseless motion. The universe is always at all points of its own cyclic evolution. There's no starting-point and no terminus, no foundation, no edge, and – let us now add – no outside either. We should at this point erase the image, because all spatio-temporal relations and all points of view are immanent *within* the process of things. There is no 'the World', because there is no point of view from which the Whole could be observed. 'The Whole' is a limit-conception. It no more designates a thing that does the phrase 'the Unknown'.

This notion of outsidelessness, and of a domain that is finite but unbounded, is a commonplace of twentieth-century thought. As we have already seen, world of *language* is finite but unbounded in a number of very obvious senses. In the one-language dictionary one word leads to another, and so on for ever. The vast strange space of linguistic meaning has no outside.

Secondly, the surface of a sphere is finite but unbounded in a way that gives us a very useful metaphor. Consider, on the surface of the Earth, the difference between the East-West axis (which has no ends, but just goes around the globe and connects up in a circle), and the North-South axis (which does have ends at the North and South poles – but when you get there you find that nothing marks them out as being different from other places). A child, hearing that the earth rotates on its axis, might suppose that the Earth actually has an axle sticking out at its axis; or, hearing about the four corners of the Earth, might suppose that the Earth ought to be pointy at the poles. But there is nothing at all special about the North Pole, except that when you are at it, it's South in all directions and North in none. There's nowhere further North to go: there's no Absolute North, straight up in the air.

Similarly – and my torus image was trying to make a similar point – there is nothing special about the Big Bang. If the Universe can be imagined as like a four-dimensional sphere, then its time-axis may be compared with the Earth's North-South axis. True, there's a moment in the endless stream of events such that all other events are later-than-it, just as there's a point on the Earth's surface such that all other points are South of it: but otherwise this always-earlier-never-later moment is quite unremarkable, and much like other points on the surface of the globe.

The persisting influence of mythological and foundationalist ways of thinking – even amongst physicists – still leads people to suppose that there is something special about the Big Bang, in such a way that its occurrence calls for explanation. And, inevitably, the explanation people want to hear will be one that postulates a great big Bloke, out there before the Big Bang, who says the word and the thing is done. But such ways of thinking can be entirely forgotten. Within the beginningless, endless and outsideless stream of fleeting events everything is constituted only by its relations with everything else. That's all: there no more needs to be a special founding Event than there needs to be a first Word or special founding Utterance to get language going.

I have spoken of the world as presenting itself, meaning that it comes forward into manifestation in the present tense, as a continuous stream of language-formed events. It is extremely dense and polyphonic and can be read in many ways. The physicist wants to read it mathematically, and a highly-introverted and artistically sensitive person wants to read it in terms of her, his, subjective feeling-responses. But most of the time and for most people the world drops quickly and habitually into our physical-object language. And why not? The world presents itself to ordinary folk not as a world of numbers, nor as the flux of our own fine-tuned intense responsive emotions, but as the interesting complicated life-world, a world of coloured, smelly, noisy, tasty physical objects. Which raises the question of the gap between the world of physical theory and the world of everyday life.

As the issue was set up in seventeenth-century philosophy, mathematical physics selected out for attention and regarded as real only those properties of bodies which could be measured and analysed mathematically. These were the so-called 'primary qualities' – size, shape, position in space, mass and velocity – which belonged objectively to bodies. By contrast, colours, noises, tastes and smells as we experience them were called 'secondary qualities', and were regarded as subjective. They were feeling-responses excited in our nervous systems by the impact of external objects upon our sensory surfaces.

This was, and is, a very unsatisfactory doctrine. I mention it here only in order to state our alternative to it. The difference between primary and secondary qualities can be replaced by the distinction between two languages: the specialized mathematical vocabulary of physics, and ordinary language. In physical theory, the difference between redness and blueness is simply a quantitative difference, that between two different wavelengths of electromagnetic radiation. In ordinary language the difference between red and blue is a literary, and therefore a qualitative, difference. The associations of 'red' with other words, and the various stock phrases into which it enters, give to redness its characteristic and complex subjective 'feel'. The same goes for 'blue'. The very different symbolic values of the two terms thus respectively condition and form our subjective experience of redness and blueness. The distinctions involved here may become prodigiously fine: anyone with a good colour sense can easily distinguish several dozens of different reds. And it is language, and only language, that can refine your palate to such a degree. Consider how, if you want to see as many greens in your garden as Pierre Bonnard could see in his, you must learn the names of the plants. So language has created colour-vision: red gets its subjectively-felt redness from the linguistic associations of the word 'red' – warmth, heat, excitement, anger, embarrassment, life, danger, sex, fire, stop. The feel of those words makes you see the redness of red: that is why we so easily speak of our moods in terms of colours. One may be yellow, feel blue, or see red. Thus on my view culture works by making us very highly, and in a very regular way, synaesthetic. The psychological aberration that the professionals call synaesthesia is only an irregular variant of everybody's normal condition.

A question now arises: why is there more than one subject of experience? Remember the fountain. The world is a continuous outpouring of language-formed events. It is dense-textured and can be read in various ways. Each language or way of reading the world picks out of the flux occurrences of its own terms and relations, and uses them to construct its own narrative about what's happening. So worlds are made: but we distinguished between the more public and objective worlds of everyday life and scientific theory that are produced on language's 'outer' face, and the worlds of subjectivity (feeling-response, desire, art) produced on language's 'inner' face. And the question is as follows: if both our physical-object language and our scientific theory construct one continuous objective world, then surely we should expect all the subjective aspects of the world similarly to join up and so become the life of one continuous superperson?

Why isn't there just one all-inclusive Subject which takes up into itself all the feeling-life of the world? Our reply will attempt to describe a novel position, intermediate between panpsychism and individualism.

I have described the world as a continuous stream of language-formed events. So intense is the communicative life of humanity that the objective world can only ever present itself already encoded within the sign-system through which it is apprehended, and subjective selfhood can know itself only within the movement of the flux of signs and relations in which it is inscribed. We have plastered over all the world with language, we ourselves are local effects of the motion of language, and the whole Earth is girdled by a ceaseless electro-magnetic hum of communication.

This reminds us that language is social, presupposing and generating a plurality of communicators who between them make up a network. It is their interaction which produces, sustains and slowly develops all meaning. In our daily communicative interaction with each other we are constantly renegotiating our delicate mutual attunement and so keeping the language alive. Consider how in every communicative expression we are both getting something off our chests and 'pressurizing' each other. That is how we seek *consensus* – shared feelings, valuations, meanings.

All this has been discussed at length elsewhere. The immediate point is that to maintain the integrity of the language and the coherence of the world, my life and yours must be deeply interwoven. There is likely to be a large overlap between the elements of the world that I connect up and incorporate into my subjective life, and the elements of the world that you connect up and incorporate into yours. Nowadays, indeed, the mass media ensure that this happens. Privacy is dead: I have very little that is mine only. Many or most philosophers in the Cartesian-empiricist tradition, from Descartes to Russell, regarded each person's experience as unique and private. The immediate objects of experience were always states of one's own sense-organs and brain. I deny that. On my account it may easily happen that elements of my visual field are simultaneously, the very same items, elements also of yours. The self is just a collection of world-events, brought into a certain specific set of relations with each other. But the act of appropriation by which, for a while, I make something mine is by no means exclusive. Lots and lots of mine may find itself simultaneously getting taken up and incorporated into you. But it doesn't follow that the life of all human subjects totalizes to become the life of one great harmonious world-soul. If that were to happen, communication would cease. A world made only of perfectly-reflective mirrors would be a world with nothing in it. For language to *live*, there have to be differences of interest and point of view. There needs to be just a little antipathy as well as sympathy. Ambivalence, we will see, is not just the spice of life, but a condition for there being any life at all. The wires between us have to be taut, or no vibrations will pass down them.

Even today there are still philosophers and preachers who idealize perfect reciprocal straightness, transparency and truth-telling in personal relationships, and who talk of love as mutual compliance. They are mistaken, because perfect compliance is merely the invisibility demanded of servants. Unless people are a little prickly, they disappear. Life and movement in our communicative relationships requires a touch of mis-understanding, provocation, duplicity, conflict of interpreta-tions, disputatiousness, teasing, malice, banter, irony and difference. Haven't you noticed? – Love is a very particular way of being irritated or stirred by someone.

It follows that there can never quite be a totalizing world-soul. Consciousness must always be finite, because it has to be consciousness *vis-à-vis* an Other: consider, for example, how your own self-consciousness is always an awareness of how you must appear in the eyes of others. The indexical pronouns teach me that to someone else I am a 'you'. So intersubjectivity is our lot, and both individualism and panpsychism are to be repudiated. And for intersubjectivity to work, we have seen, two conditions must be fulfilled: first, the self must be completely brought down into the flux of language-formed events that is the world, so that it can be seen as a temporary collection, an aggregate, a 'time being' born of the flux and returning at last into it. Thus understood, selves can overlap. They have, they are *in*, common ground. And secondly, each self must also be aware of having its own interest in life and point of view. A little difference or otherness between selves is needed. It gives to utterances their force, and keeps language alive. What is variously described as 'pressurizing', 'needling' and 'working on' someone is a feature of all human interactions, and we should not make the mistake of supposing that it can somehow be evaded, overcome or transcended. Sameness is death, Otherness life. A bit of the Other is good for you: you need it, so don't complain about it.

Can we now put together an account of how things are with us that is consistent with the best available modern systems of knowledge, and also consistent with itself? Not easy – so beware of what follows.

The universe is pictured as a vast slow-motion explosion, scattering radiation and tiny packets of energy across space and time. What these packets or particles consist in, what their 'nature' is, cannot be said very clearly; but they can be and are modelled mathematically. In the stars material is compressed at very high energy-levels, whereas in empty space it is distributed at a density of only about one hydrogen atom per cubic metre. But where there is sufficient material at a low enough energy-level, as in the planets, the heavier elements, molecules and in due course more complex objects can appear and persist.

Some of these more complex objects have the striking

property of maintaining themselves for a while by extracting energy from their immediate environment. Certain tropical storms fuel themselves in this way, and because they may keep their identity for a week or two as they traverse several thousand miles of ocean, meteorologists name them. But the outstanding examples of self-maintaining and self-replicating objects are of course living organisms – which raises a difficult question. Nobody would wish to attribute a will to live to hurricanes, but living things are another matter. Many people still feel that a purely mechanistic vocabulary cannot be quite adequate in biology. They feel the need to postulate some sort of conative drive that makes the creature struggle to live and to pass on its genes, and can account for the fact that instead of stopping with bacteria (which surely are already as successful as any creature could be) the evolutionary process has pushed on to produce organisms of greater and greater complexity and fragility.

At just this point Schopenhauer thought we could break out of the order of representation and contact something 'deeper'. He calls it 'the Will'. Introspection, he maintains, can show us something of what the Will is, and in living things we can recognize the effects of its operation out-there in the phenomenal world. So Schopenhauer waxes metaphysical about the Will – as I too have sought a unifying image of the energy that moves us, moves language and moves in our world. But I talk only myth, for there are reasons to be cautious, because the history of science indicates that science has in general been most successful when it has stuck most closely to a mechanistic vocabulary. So I do not claim more than that a particular manner of speaking is useful and sheds some light on the way we tick and the way other living organisms tick.

A living organism, then, is a cluster of natural phenomena so ordered that it behaves as a single self-regulating system. No occult life-principle need be postulated, but an organism has an interest in life, and events in its environment mean something to it in so far as they may affect its life-prospects. And for many other creatures, as for us humans, what most effectively galvanizes an organism into activity is *ambivalence*, which we

66

may define in a preliminary way as a divergence of aim or a conflict between forces within the individual organism. Perhaps no sentient, motile animal can quite avoid ambivalence. For the animal must strive to maintain its own life, but it must also strive to give life to the next generation even if at the cost of its own life. And a further ambivalence arises in relation to sexual reproduction, for humans and other animals perhaps always find that the Other is at once intensely attractive and also alien and threatening.

Ambivalent impulses can be extremely strong and disturbing to the organism – which is perhaps one of the reasons why so much ritualization and symbolic exchange commonly come to surround the stressful business of animal territoriality, court-ship, pair-bonding and the care of the young. It is thought that excessive excitation may sometimes be discharged by irrelevant-seeming behaviours, as when a courting sea-bird suddenly stops and preens for a while before resuming – a 'displacement activity'. Subsequently the preening-episode may become a regular part of the courtship ritual.

At any rate, during the forty years or so since the notion of language-games became part of the currency, it has become clear that a great many animals are highly Wittgensteinian. Each symbolic behaviour is part of a game played in a certain life-situation, functioning in such a way as to help the creature to succeed in its life-task. It needs to survive, but it cannot be alone all the time. At least during the breeding season, it needs to rub along with other members of its own species, and it needs to transmit its genes. Its 'language' guides it through the behaviours it must execute in order to succeed in these aims whilst also maintaining the stability both of the individual organism and of social relationships within the breeding group.

Animal communications may have more than one meaning. We need not dwell here on the duplicitous behaviour that may be employed, for example, by a hunter stalking its prey, or by an animal that mimics the behaviour of something else less appetizing than itself. Our present concern is with cases where an animal's behaviour seems to be expressing and relieving ambivalent feelings. Thus in its courtship behaviour an animal may be signalling its readiness to mate, its desire to mollify an aggressive partner, its intention to calm and reassure a fearful partner, or extreme aggression on its own part – and so on. So highly-excitable a matter is courtship that one and the same piece of behaviour may be discharging several different but equally strong impulses simultaneously.

This suggests three general theses that bear upon the origin of human language. The whole reproductive cycle tends to give rise to strongly ambivalent feelings. Secondly, *the sign is a compromise-formation*: that is, a great many or even most symbolic behaviours are shaped by the individual's need to find channels through which conflicting feelings can be relieved simultaneously. And thirdly, as Freud's dream-book long ago showed us, sexuality and reproduction is the area of life in which our feelings are most ambivalent and the production of signs is most intensive.

All this indicates how, by developing the legacies of Darwin, Freud and Wittgenstein, we may in due course be able to give a fully naturalistic account of what human language is. In playing our various language-games, we too are channelling and discharging our energies, building and maintaining our complex social worlds, and generally furthering the purposes of life.

So there seems to be a possibility of telling a continuous story, with no nasty jumps or gaps in it, of how the world of nature has gradually evolved into the world of culture. There is one continuous spreading outflow of world-energies. Over aeons of time it has happened to give rise to small eddies which keep their shape and even multiply. Extracting energy from their environment, they behave as if (for a while) they have a life of their own. So they are living things. And some of their borrowed energies may be expended through symbolic behaviours that help them to fulfil their life-aims.

Various complications, however, have already appeared, and will need further discussion. The general drift of all things is toward ever-greater entropy, and we have described a living organism as being, like an eddy in a river, a temporary and local reversal of the general downhill drift of everything. By synthesizing our own food, or by eating other organisms, we living things are able for a little while to extract enough energy from the flux to enable us to stand up against it, until in due course we merge back into the flux from which we first arose.

Now, if we were fully-unified and consistent systems, all of whose energies were harnessed and guided so as consistently to pull in the same direction, we might have language but we would not have self-consciousness. It would not be needed, because it would have no function. Like many animals, we could employ a symbolic behaviour to face down a rival, win a mate or mark our territory without thinking about it – i.e., without ambivalence, and therefore without ambiguity, and therefore without consciousness. And indeed, that is how it is with most of us for much of the time: we run through much of our daily routine 'without thinking about it' – i.e., at a very low level of conscious awareness.

However, we are not fully unified and consistent systems. We incorporate a great many subsystems which may pull in different directions. Such contrary impulses are apparent even in animal behaviour, anticipating our human psychomachy. I have already mentioned the most important of these conflicting pairs of drives. We desire to affirm life, but we also passionately yearn for death. We desire to preserve our own lives, but we also want to communicate life to the next generation and to yield our place to them. We long for union with the Other, but the Other (*as* Other) appears to us threatening and even repulsive. We may feel both tender and aggressive impulses within ourselves, directed towards the same object.

Whenever we are taken aback and whenever we deliberate, we may become aware of conflicting forces or energies within ourselves. But if ambivalence is present, it will come through into our symbolic expression as semantic ambiguity whether we are consciously aware of 'sending out conflicting signals' or not. In which case it is to the addressee's advantage that he or she should possess the skill of reading the ambiguous signal and responding to it appropriately.

Self-consciousness, then, is a space opened up by the operation of conflicting forces within the body. It is an interpretative skill, in so far as it is biologically advantageous to us that we shall become so attuned to others that we learn to read in the signs they give off the conflicting forces at work within their systems. And consciousness involves sym-pathy, co-feeling, in so far as my own system may resonate with, and also recognize, the vibrations given off by another. So self-consciousness, and with it the construction of a highly differentiated 'mental' or psychic world, is a highly social matter. It functions to bind us together into a community of people who feel alike and feel for each other, and can therefore understand each other.

In the main tradition of Western philosophical and religious thought it was just about always maintained – at least up to Darwin – that there could be a completely unified, uncomplicated and blessed spiritual selfhood, the selfhood of a person whose self-expression is lucid and straight, with no contrary undercurrents or hidden agenda. Such model persons might include God, angels, saints, philosophers and righteous people generally.

But our argument has pointed to the opposite conclusion. A human being is a very complex system with a great many subsystems. It is possible for us at times to be so absorbed and happy that we are not aware of any internal conflicts at all; but at these moments we are unconscious. Consciousness as such is always, amongst other things, a cry of pain, and some measure of disequilibrium within the body is apparent in every human symbolic expression, linguistic or behavioural. Whatever you are saying or doing, there's always something hidden for psychoanalysis, or its more up-to-date successor deconstruction, to bring to light.

At this point the doctrine of meaning needs to be somewhat changed. In general, animal senses are geared to the perception not of identities but of differences. A grazing mammal is very bad at identifying objects, but responds almost instantly to the tiniest movement in its field of view – a movement being a difference. Similarly, and generalizing, if you are acutely responsive to other people's body-language and utterances, then what you are most sensitive to is not the frequency and amplitude of one particular vibration that someone else gives off, but rather a certain jangling, discordance or dissonance within the vibes that they give off. So a meaning is a felt discordance, a slight jangle that the hearer feels and feels with.

Human being is thus an experience of conflict of forces and resulting pain. Freud treats only the neurotic symptom as a compromise-formation, but on the view proposed here the sign as such is a compromise-formation. It is produced at the moment when we try to express ourselves, and is heard as a slight jangling discord between the two different wavelengths that we are trying to get out into unified utterance. I can never quite make what I'm trying to say completely harmonious. People who have sensitive ears detect the faint jangling in what I say. They ask, 'What conflicting forces are producing this jangling?'; and that is the starting-point for a powerful analytical or deconstructive interpretation of what I am saying. Nor should such an interpretation be seen as sceptical or reductive. On the contrary, it involves precisely *sympathy*, a sympathy which co-feels all the undercurrents.

Compare this with FM radio. The top line, the frequency that is transmitted continuously, carries no message at all. The whole of the message is carried in the modulation, the slightly jangling departures from the norm. So the receiver listens to the modulation, not to the main frequency – and that is how it is with human beings, too.

Earlier, it was stated that the whole world of subjectivity is produced on the 'inner' face of language. I have now elucidated that claim somewhat. Remember, the aim is to give as truthful and naturalistic an account of the world, the human self and language as possible. The world, then, is the fountain, a slow-motion explosion of tiny scattering energies. A living organism is a complex collection of these energies, so arranged as to form a temporarily self-maintaining system. By extracting energy from its environment it finds the strength for a while to resist the general drift of all things towards dissolution and uniformity. It can even reproduce itself. However, the more complex living organisms contain many subsystems, not always perfectly harmonized; and all living organisms are subject to a certain conflict of aims. For there to have been an evolution of life *at all*, each living thing must be programmed to struggle to maintain its own life, and for there to be an evolution of life *at all*, each living thing must struggle to pass on its genes to the next generation and then give place to it. Thus some degree of ambivalence has entered into the project of life from its beginning. It is revealed everywhere in the symbolic behaviours by which the more complex animals regulate their social and reproductive lives, and is the dominant factor in culture, which is the sphere of human life. Although in general our social life and language-games are clearly just more complex versions of very similar behaviours to be seen amongst animals, human life is pervaded by psychic discord to such a degree that the whole world of symbolic meaning and subjective life is touched by it. Every meaning can be felt as a faint discord, every utterance or text has a subtext, all consciousness is in some degree painful. – And, by the way, if you doubt this last point, then attend closely to the strange sensation of yearning, grief and near-tearfulness that accompanies even the most exalted happiness and enjoyment that we can experience.

All of which gives rise to the next problem. We sought as naturalistic and therefore truthful an account as could be got of selfhood, consciousness and language. I have outlined the form it will take. But if it ends by making all human utterance merely symptomatic and expressive, then it applies to itself and negates itself. Besides which, are not our opening paragraphs in trouble, because they purport to describe in language states of things long, long before there could possibly have been any language? We began by making the minimum entity in our metaphysics some language-formed event or difference. But how can a string of human signs represent a state of the world before there were any human signs around to form events?

Perhaps our account is reflexively paradoxical in the way that the word *chaos*, formless chaos, is paradoxical. For chaos is the word we use for the unthinkable pre-verbal state of things.

So we need now to say how language produces the objective world on its outer face, and how far a world thus conjured up by language may legitimately be projected out in space, or backwards in time.

How, then, is a language in its use able to conjure up a world? An obvious starting-point might be a literary text such as an ancient play, which reaches us with no stage-directions. 'Realizing' the text, actors call its world into being.

This example, however, is objectionable. Both the actors and we the audience are in such a case merely situating the text in a highly-elaborated world-picture that we have already got. We are certainly *not* making an entirely fresh start and allowing the text to create its own world out of nothing. Indeed, in such a case one cannot do so.

A stronger example, then, might be the case of a Victorian traveller who makes the first-ever contact with an exotic tribe. No translator is present. He has to learn their language and culture from the beginning and he does so – which is a considerable achievement. But he can do it because he successfully presumes a good deal of common ground. All human communities have languages, and all natural human languages have a large number of structural features and powers in common. The explorer can therefore get away with the parochial earthling assumption that the way their tongue builds their world for them will turn out to have much in common with the way his European language builds his world for him. So, again, he's not really starting from scratch. (Notice, too, that human sign-language and body-language are extremely ancient and have much in common all around the world.)

What about the case of a mime like Marcel Marceau, who uses no words at all and invents much of his own body-language? True, his gestures do seem to bring into being the physical objects that he bumps into, handles, eats or whatever; but he is not creating *ex nihilo*. On the contrary, he gives pleasure precisely because he re-minds us of our own construction and experience of bodiliness in a bodily world. He gives pleasure, not by creating something new for us, but by drawing what we already know out of us.

So we turn to a stronger and clearer example, our attempt to learn how an animal through its behaviours shapes its life and constructs its world. Imagine that you spend three or four summer months for several years in succession with a colony of breeding seabirds. Cut out your human construction of your human world, especially the *seen* world. Simplify the perceived world down to the biologically-necessary signals that trigger behaviours. Your mate is a black-and-white pattern on a head, with a dab of red at the base of the bill; your nest-site is a very simple pencil-scrawled visual pattern; your rival is a bit of bobbing threat-behaviour; the predatory kittiwake that threatens your chicks is just a visual pattern that triggers a jump of alarm; your chicks are squawks and yellow gapes; your prey appears only as what a human might call a flicker at the corner of one's eye.

It is a very minimal visual world. You don't have a human-type world-picture. You see only as much as is biologically-significant, so that everything seen is just a stimulus, arousing a prompt and even vehement behavioural response. Your auditory world is very rich: you can easily distinguish the voices of your own mate and your own chicks from the crowd, even at some distance. But this too is a matter of the sensory apparatus being directed entirely towards what is biologically-significant. One might similarly observe that most human beings, for most of human history, have paid attention only to what is economically, medicinally, socially or ritually significant to them.

To return to our seabird-watching, the task is to bracket-out one's own subjectivity so far as possible and to observe as closely as one can, year after year, all the successive stages of the breeding-cycle. The bird is a complex, trembling, self-regulating system of energies, preprogrammed with (as we have argued earlier) a slightly-discordant group of life-aims. It is highly sensitive to stimuli, and has appropriate behavioural responses already inbuilt.

Now these behaviours include symbolic behaviours which convey messages, for example to a rival, to a chick, or to a prospective mate. The signs involved have important properties. They are general forms through which the bird can express itself and discharge its slightly-discordant impulses, as when threat-behaviour expresses strong anxiety and aggression at once. And the signs, being general, can also be recognized by, and communicate something to, the addressee. Furthermore the signs, also by being general, allude to other occasions when they were used or might be used. There was (to pursue the present example) a similar confrontation with a rival an hour ago, and another one yesterday. The generality of the sign thus lifts the bird a little out of total immersion in the battle of the present moment and allows it to do what it needs to do and does do – learn from experience.

Birds differ from each other somewhat in degree of dominance, and in other aspects of behaviour too. I have suggested that this is because the universal biological fact of ambivalence gives to every complex animal a highly differentiated and graduated 'emotional' life. So there are recognizable distinct 'personalities' – as all really close observers find. As a result social animals, interacting each with its neighbours, may generate a complex social world.

I do not wish in a realistic sense to attribute subjective consciousness to birds, because (as I have shown elsewhere) subjective consciousness is a mythical notion. For the next step in the present argument we need only a more modest formulation. Suppose that an experienced and close observer studies the expressive behavioural language of a particular species of seabird, and then follows an individual through the entire breeding season, then one can understand what it means to say that language has an inner face which is subjectivity, for in its whole behaviour the bird has constructed and manifested an individual 'personality' and has fulfilled its own life-aim. And by the same token, the breeding colony has taught us how it collectively constructs its own social world.

The breeding gulls show us, then, the sense in which every

complex social animal, through its biologically-evolved behaviour patterns and language-games, constructs both distinguishable individuals and a common social world of its own. It is to be noticed, though, that the bird's whole ethology is specific to it. It does not know *the* world; *it builds its own world* – subject to very close biological constraints. We need not for one moment suggest that its world is illusory, but it is important to be clear that its whole worldview is highly functional. The bird sees, hears, scents and so on only what it needs to take note of if it is to survive. And since the survival-requirements of different species are different, they construct different worlds.

In the light of this example, what are we to make of the very great diversity of human languages and cultures? A few things at least are clear. Every human being lives within a cultural world. A cultural world consists of a complex system of signs, narratives and historically-evolved language-games, within which each of us is assigned a social position, constructs a form of selfhood and participates in a socially-constructed objective world. The constraints governing the construction of the world are not by any means purely biological. They are in a broad sense cultural, having to do with *cultus*. They are concerned with the link between *cosmos* and *ethos*. Traditional narratives prescribe a vision of the cosmic order, a (related) vision of the social order, and *therefore* a way of life. We noticed the ritual organization of space and time in the case of our seabirds, for with them too there are behaviours appropriate to specific locations and seasons of the year. But in the human case there are often founding cosmological narratives laying down what is to be done, when and where. This, no doubt, is what gave to us our much stronger sense of participating in and re-enacting an endlessly reiterating sacred round through which everything returns into its own origin and is refreshed and renewed. Such mythic validation of our form of life makes humans rather strongly inclined to 'realism', the innocent belief that our own cultural signs and myths somehow represent objectively real beings, in such a way that *our* world is, we think, *the* world absolutely. In our own age of ethnicity

76

and fundamentalism it has become apparent that a great many people still live within their own traditional cultural world, with all its local overbeliefs, and naïvely suppose it to be *the* world absolutely.

In terms of our own argument, however, every traditional cultural world that human beings have made is only a local world with its own internal sort of objectivity. And it can still be viewed entirely as a natural product. We humans differ from the lesser black-backed gull and the rest in that we are much more highly-strung. Our drives are more painfully ambivalent, more finely differentiated and graduated. Because (as I said earlier) subjectivity is the inner face and objectivity the outer face of language, with the three realms – of feeling, of language and of the world – being precisely coterminous, it follows that our fragile emotional balance is reflected in the greater complexity of our language-games and their openness to modification, and *also* in the much greater complexity of our constructed objective worlds.

This, by the way, creates a further paradox. I said that we are emotionally ambivalent, fragile, divided animals. Our personal cohesion as individual systems and our social cohesion are often precarious. We are *cosmically* restless, anxious and insecure – with the bizarre consequence that on the one hand we change our culture and way of life far more rapidly than any other animal species could possibly do, whilst on the other hand we constantly repeat stories that trace our way of life back to its source in a timeless and perfect world above.

We are tragic and riven animals – and therefore have to be culturally productive in order to survive. Hopelessly restless, we have to change very fast, while simultaneously nourishing ourselves with fictions of an unchanging objective truth, reality and value.

That, however, is not the end of the story, for the final twist is that our human rivenness is a *felix culpa*, a happy fault. For because we are divided, the world can be united. Because we are divided we are supersensitive, painfully conscious, culturally productive and story-telling beings. Because we are ambivalent about life and death, sameness and otherness, self-preservation and self-abandonment, we tell cosmic stories by which we seek to place our life within a frame that will sustain it and make it intelligible.

Stories – like this one. For we began by defining the world as a continuous flux of language-formed events. In that case, whose language formed the remote prehuman past? Ours, and it has done so only recently. The scientific story that we now tell has been developed as a sort of possibility-condition. Present-day ways of describing the world, when analysed, require us to tell such-and-such a story about the past. Logically, our present construction of the world comes first, and our cosmic narrative is secondary. Our capacity to verbalize and so finish the world thus, as it were, circles back to the beginning and makes the Big Bang and cosmic evolution real in retrospect. Religious thought may picture God as having used human language to make it all real contemporaneously. But in fact we are speaking of events which, by definition, could not have been described-and-observed by anybody, and therefore have had to wait for a strange retroactive realization, given to them by us in modern scientific theory.

So we are advocating a queer sort of scientific realism after all. Within your visual field at this moment world-stuff takes on a languagey organization, brightness and order which if you were not in the room it would not have. As the ancient myth says, it is language that turns chaos into cosmos. The world becomes finished as we describe it. This is what Heidegger called *lichtung*, the lighting-up of beings by language, a work that Being does in and through us.[7] Some scientists have marvelled that, in our becoming conscious and then developing modern science, the Universe has become conscious of itself. But this consciousness is not something superadded upon an ante-cedently finished cosmos: it is the world's becoming Cosmos. So during the present century physics has brought to life the Big Bang, the formation of the galaxies and the early history of the earth. It is all becoming real in retrospect. It is a back-projection, humankind's greatest work of art.

In some such sense as this, Nietzsche has described the world as a work of art that continually gives birth to itself. In your visual field, now, is the evidence that he's right.

Because we are divided, the world is united. As we have seen, the project of life is inescapably a little at odds with itself from the outset. For life cannot evolve unless the individual living organism is so ordered as to maintain its own integrity: that is, it must (metaphorically speaking, at least) 'struggle' for existence. But it must also struggle successfully to pass on its genes and then by dying to make way for the next generation.

We cannot just struggle for ourselves; we also struggle *to be succeeded*. So the reproductive drive is and has to be both Eros and Thanatos, that is, both sex-drive and death-wish. Approaching orgasm, and perhaps especially when giving birth, we must and do cast ourselves adrift, floating carelessly towards our own death in order to affirm life.

There is thus a touch of ambivalence in the very project of life, and in the more complex organisms it starts to show in their expressive and communicative symbolic behaviours. In human beings ambivalence develops into consciousness, and signing into language. The result is that we develop through our social intercourse a prodigiously complex social world, a world made of language. Our feeling-response to the movement of world-energies within our systems and impinging upon us becomes so finely-differentiated that it colours up the world, gives it objectivity, makes it real, *finishes* it, to yield the world we see. (And to make possible the back-projected and metaphorical theory of the world and the self that you now read.)

Attend to your own visual field. In a sense already specified, you see phrases, words, theories. That is, you see – or at least, I see at this moment – a yellow book on a white shelf, sunlight. So you are seeing language; or (we may say) you are seeing a language-formed movement of energies, as the super-delicate play of emotions upon the interface between you and the world expresses itself in a dance of signs. That is reality coming into being in your perception of it – the true, the philosophical,

Big Bang happening even now, in the flux of language-formed events tingling upon your sensory surfaces.

Thus we become the first *cosmological* creatures. The project of life was a little ambivalent from its inception. In us the ambivalence becomes so acute and painful as to create consciousness. The rush of our very-finely modulated feelings, pouring out into symbolic expression, structures and colours up the visual field. So the real objective world generated on the outside of language gets to be as fabulously rich and complex as the play of our feelings. From microcosm through logos to macrocosm, the Word constantly mediates between subjectivity and the Universe. There's a fountain in us too, Eros/Thanatos, matching the cosmological fountain that we have postulated.

So, as I said, it is because we are so divided that the world is united. The world, our human world, becomes real in and through our own expressive-emotive-symbolic response to it and writing of it. Our rivenness then is a happy fault, *felix culpa*. But the human being need not be left just twitching in pain. There is now a second movement to be made in order to complete the cycle. It is the movement of redemption, to be called *ecstatic immanence*.

On 26 April 1336, the young Petrarch wrote a letter reporting that he had just climbed Mount Ventoux in Provence, to see the view.[8] Not to pray or to sacrifice but merely to see the view, so that the letter is sometimes quoted – inaccurately, as we shall see – as marking the beginning of the Renaissance turn to this world.

Petrarch excuses his action in various ways. He finds a precedent in Livy, who has reported that Philip of Macedon once climbed a mountain to reconnoitre a theatre of planned military operations. Petrarch is careful to stress the disagreeableness of the climb, as if he doesn't want us to think he's having much fun, and he only briefly describes the vast panorama to be seen from the summit. Can it be right to spend so long in mere earthly enjoyment? He takes out the small copy of Augustine's *Confessions* that he always carries with him, and opens it by chance, or so he claims, at the passage (X.8.15) where the saint speaks of those who seek out the wonders of Nature, mountains, oceans, rivers – and desert themselves.

Petrarch is stunned and ashamed that he still admires earthly things. He descends the mountain absorbed in religious reflections. The things to be seen by the inner eye of the mind are infinitely nobler than the things to be seen by the carnal eye. We should be treading down our passions in the ascent of the mind to God, rather than indulging them by climbing a mere pile of rocks. With these improving thoughts Petrarch closes his letter, and leaves the reader suspecting that the whole expedition has been merely a literary fiction. The only sign that the Renaissance is coming has been the way Petrarch has exercised his ego, rather than his body.

Although indeed he has said nothing of interest about landscape, Petrarch does say one interesting thing about his own feelings at the summit. He reports feelings of yearning. There is a whiff here of what will in due course come to be discussed as the sublime. When we are overwhelmed by visual beauty in nature or in art, it is as if we wish to drown in it, or as if we wish to pass out into and dissolve away in our own visual field. I want to die into the absolute immanence that I am, that I make. Hence what I called 'ecstatic immanence', for this is indeed a purely immanent rapture, when sense-experience, the dance of signs as I have described it, becomes so powerful that it drains us of all our painful ambivalent feelings, and we are blissfully emptied out into the world that we are making. This may happen as we are making something in clay or wood or paint; and it may also happen in ordinary perception. For perception too is on our account an expressive, symbolic *activity*.

The experience we have been describing blurs the received distinctions between nature and art, and between aesthetic production and aesthetic contemplation. And why not? Much of Renaissance thought, it seems, did something very similar; and so too did Romanticism.

Over forty years ago I saw, in England, the Camberwell Beauty, *Nymphalis antiopa* – something extraordinary. But there was no such experience before 1748, when the first two were taken in Camberwell – or perhaps it should be 1766, when the butterfly was first described and illustrated in *The Aurelian* of Moses Harris. Since then there have been a few years in which it has been not uncommon – 1789, 1846, 1872, 1880, 1947 and 1976. To see it, I think in 1947, was a wonderful experience, a peak of childhood, never to be forgotten. But the beauty and the wonder of seeing this particular species in England was and is a literary and historical creation. In its Scandinavian home the same species is not the Camberwell Beauty and is not uncommon. Seeing it is nothing remarkable.

Before the mid-seventeenth century few insects were remarked at all, except perhaps as moral emblems. Bees and ants might typify industry, frugality and the social virtues; and butterflies? – the 'gilded fly' might represent frivolous, transient earthly beauty. Nothing to love or to wonder at: all of which is a reminder of what a great cultural and religious achievement the making of the scientific gaze has been. The eye needs intensive literary training, and science is even better than painting as a training for the eye. Our perception is formed by a huge volume of taxonomical description, observations, biological theory and so on. Generations of accumulated literary work have made seeing a butterfly what it is today. Historical geographers have taught us to read the history of landscape as we look at it, and we are getting into the habit of reading the history of the rocks and the very heavens.

By and large, people are not yet ready to acknowledge the extent to which the world we see around us today is a literary creation. I urge them to consider the following analogy: the process by which a new biological species comes to be registered and recognized is very similar to the process by which a new invention comes to be registered and patented in the name of its inventor. In each case the new object that you have found-or-made (Latin, *invenire*) needs to be named, described in the proper technical vocabulary, approved by an official scrutineer as original, and duly registered. In each case, the inventor (in the Latin sense) feels a certain parental pride – as one of my own science teachers, the botanist Oleg Polunin, took a great and justifiable pride in having given his name to several plants and a frog. Petrarch's misfortune was that, although he was a word-man, the natural world in his day had not yet been *described*. It was little better than a barren wilderness.

All this means that we cannot possibly now disparage visual experience in the way Petrarch still did. The scientific gaze (we are talking about the observational sciences, and especially about the life sciences and the human, behavioural sciences) is a great cultural and religious achievement which has vastly enriched the world and is capable of healing the self. So what was going wrong in Petrarch's case?

Petrarch presumably began with the ordinary human condition, a disequilibrium of the body forces. My argument has been that in this case the path to salvation must be through a style of expressive symbolic activity which simultaneously purges our conflicting feelings and enriches the objective world. Examples of such therapeutic action might be artistic creation, productive work, ritual and even (trained and attentive) sense-perception. But Petrarch lived in a culture still predominantly ascetical. Asceticism is a cultural movement that aims to heighten consciousness by entrenching and even exacerbating the disequilibrium and conflict of forces within the body, and then, so to say, taking sides in a struggle for mastery. Asceticism works by fixing in the language a whole series of value-laden binary oppositions – flesh versus spirit, outer versus inner, dispersal versus recollection, surface versus depth, sense versus reason and so on. The individual finds himself or herself pressured into frequent displays of preference for the second of each of these pairs; and that is what Petrarch duly provides. He makes all the right noises because he needs to please the master to whom he writes, a professor of theology. Very ugly they sound, but then, religion in Petrarch's time was extremely confused. It said: the word has become flesh, therefore we must despise the flesh. That was – perhaps still is – orthodoxy. In those days it had real power. In retrospect, one wonders how it could ever have seemed to make sense.

Yet Petrarch is full of these absurdities. As he climbs he gets lost, and sits down to rest. 'There I leapt in my winged thoughts from things corporeal to what is incorporeal' – and inevitably he draws a contrast between the present journey, made 'with the feet of my body ... the frail body that is doomed to die', and life's real task, the journey of 'the agile and immortal mind' to God. So a Christian who climbs a mountain ought to occupy himself with thoughts of what an absurd thing he is doing, and how comparatively worthless the body is anyway. In the end the only profit Petrarch has from the ascent of Mount Ventoux is the realization that he has wasted his time. Amen to that, for he has wasted our time too. One is grateful for the Renaissance, for the painter's eye, for the scientific gaze, for the rehabilitation of the body and of Nature, and most of all perhaps for the dissolving away of mind-body dualism. The body is a complex system of energies with many sub-systems, maintaining its equilibrium by constantly expressing itself, coming forth into representation as a dance of signs. The fountain that we are. So the mind is just the body's own ever-changing symbolic expression. The notion of the flesh as heavy and inert, a drag upon the soul, is quite wrong. The flesh is quick, animate, expressive, communicative. And we are fleshwords.

In the account I have been giving it has been, I hope, clear that the life-world, the body and the observational sciences are all being understood non-realistically. Ordinary perception is a sort of reading. Just at this moment, looking up, I see again that yellow book sitting on the white-painted bookshelf. So my perception coincided with the activation of a little chain of linguistic signs, with numerous side-chains of association running off it. The yellow is the yellow of lemon peel, a little greenish and sharp, not quite as motherly as butter. And so on: side-chains, many of them. Anyhow, the life-world is a flux, a dense matted texture of language-formed events. It takes on clarity and order when studied from a particular angle, with a certain interest in mind. An observational science is a community, an interest-group of people schooled to look at a certain subject-matter in a certain way, picking out of it a certain descriptive vocabulary and style of theorizing. But there is no very sharp discontinuity between their ways of speaking and ordinary language. All social training or education pressures us to look at the flux with some special interest in mind, and to select out of it a single line of well-made prose. Ordinary experience, so-called 'thought', is a babble, linguistically too excessive to make any clear sense. Training reduces it, boils it down, *selects* a line of meaningfulness out of it.

But what about mathematical physics, the most beautiful and highly-developed of the sciences, and the one furthest removed from ordinary language? I have in the account given so far borrowed some vocabulary and imagery from physics, talking of energies, forces and a scattering explosion, and this may suggest that perhaps a realistic account may be given of physics when it gets completed and fully mathematized. It will then be the science of primary qualities, the one fundamental science of nature – with bits of chemistry and biophysics added to it, so far as they too have become completely mathematized. The observational sciences, tied to the life-world and to natural language, will then be regarded as sciences of the secondary, emotion-coloured, verbalized world.

No. We cannot quite allow a special status to mathematical physics, because mathematical signs are still just signs; and how can a mathematical calculus or scheme carry with it, or generate just out of itself, the knowledge that it does apply to something else quite distinct from itself?

René Descartes, setting up the modern project of mathematical physics, reduced a material body just to its own geometry. So what's the difference between a cubic metre of marble and a cubic metre of empty space? To avoid the difficulty, Descartes denied the vacuum. All space is occupied. The distinction between empty and filled space does not arise in his system of the world. But a feeling of puzzlement remains. If the material world, the world of primary qualities, is *just* a lot of Euclidean geometry containing a lot of mechanical motions, then what's the difference between a world that exists only abstractly in the calculations of mathematicians and one that exists also concretely? There doesn't seem to be any. All Descartes can do is invoke a gut-feeling, an innate conviction we all have that there is a real world, and he claims that since God is not a deceiver we may assume that he would not have created us with this conviction unless it were veridical. And it is evident, says Descartes, that God has the power to create such a world. So there is one.

Strikingly, Descartes has in effect made realism about the external material world a matter, in the end, of gut-feeling and religious faith and no more. Why does Descartes think the issue important at all? I think, only the fact that he is such a strong mind/matter dualist. He needs to be reassured that his mathematical physics is not 'merely' a conceptual scheme, but is also incarnated objectively in the order of a material world that exists independently of his mind. He needs to feel that his mathematical scheme is true of something. Thus mind/matter dualism leads people to worry about whether their thoughts or their language are accurately representing the (supposedly-independent) facts out-there.

On our account such worries do not arise. The flux of already-sign-formed events exists in a realm *anterior* to the making of any distinction between what's going on out there in the world, and what's going on in here in the mind. The flux I described spans and incorporates language *and* reality, the 'inner' world of thoughts *and* the 'outer' world of being. We simply do not yet make (and anyway, I never want to make) the old ugly distinctions between mind and matter, word and thing, thought and being. And because I don't want to make such distinctions, I don't want the correspondence theory of truth. I don't want to say that a science is like a map, and needs in addition to itself a real world of which it is the map. We don't need a two-decker metaphysics, which distinguishes the order of objective reality from the order of its representation. There's only that dense tangled flux in which those with the right training find the traces of mathematical concepts and relationships. So of mathematical physics we need to say only that it strives to achieve internal self-consistency, and freedom from (at least from any gross or inexplicable) inconsistency with our construction of the ordinary-language world. When we say that a scientific theory is 'true', we say only that it can safely be relied upon, because no circumstances have yet been found in which it turns out to be misleading. Modern physical theory is no doubt a highly-specialized way of reading highly-selected bits of the world, but so far as it goes it makes excellent sense. It has provided us with some very good images. So there's no reason for antirealism to be anti-science, as so many people have mistakenly supposed. On the contrary, the anti-realist account of what the natural sciences are doing stresses the enormous imaginative enrichment of our world-picture that they have brought. Not dogmatic knowledge of the world absolutely, but enrichment of our world-picture. Compared with any modern biologist, Petrarch stumbled about half-blind. He doesn't name one animal, or one plant, or even one kind of rock. In his day most things were not yet named.

Until very recently, consciousness was almost always the consciousness of subjection. The self was situated in the world feeling a little awkward, nervous and not quite understanding what was happening, like a sixteen-year-old girl just entering service or an eighteen-year-old boy entering the Army. You found yourself in the care of a great, powerful and mysterious institution which expected you, had a place for you and had its eye upon you. It was often cruel and arbitrary in its operation, but it provided a complete way of life. Its power overarched everything. What it said, went. It fixed meanings, it controlled truth, it laid down all the rules and it gave you your task. You could not penetrate to the centre of it, and you could not argue with it. Structural change was almost unthinkable, but if it were to happen it could be brought about only from Higher Up. What went on Higher Up you did not know; it was far beyond your ken. Your task was only to obey. You did not wish to attract attention to yourself; you hoped only to fit in so perfectly as to pass unnoticed.

Until very recently, almost all our institutions – political, religious, academic, military and so on – were of this type. Terms like 'a good soldier', 'a good wife', 'a good student' and so on gained their special resonance from the general assumption that human life must be lived within great disciplinary institutions that prescribe roles, control truth and lay down the rules. Franz Kafka is perhaps the most moving example of a person who found himself inexplicably quite unable to do and to be what was 'institutionally' expected of him. But he was very exceptional. To this day many human beings remain intensely nostalgic for and committed to the old disciplinary and institutional vision of the world and of how human life should be lived. Its intellectual formulation is *realism*, the belief that everything we should live by and within is antecedently fixed and real out-there – meanings, Truth, rules of life, and the Cosmos itself and our own 'place' within it. Metaphysical realism, Kafka's Castle, has been humanity's reference-point for millennia. We are thoroughly institutionalized within it, so much so that even in North America very few people can yet bear to consider life outside it. In Britain, of course, Kafka's Castle is falling down. Beyond repair now. In slightly hysterical, accusing voices people are blaming each other for its disintegration, and demanding that it be rebuilt.

The antirealist vision of life is a vision of life no longer lived under the shadow of the old Castle. And damned odd it is indeed, so odd that it is very difficult to give an orderly linear account of it. Let's begin with another image, the potter. When we are absorbed in life we are like a potter at the wheel. Mind-matter dualism and subject-object dualism are not to be thought of. They don't arise. The potter is completely given to or poured out into the work that engages her, and the clay is completely plastic to her. So, metaphysically, the world is a continuous, very plastic flux of language-formed events, in which are we totally immersed, in such a way that the more completely we can forget our former fancied metaphysical dignity and be content simply to give ourselves into life, the more completely the world is given to us. Total concentration in childlike creative play is blissfully mindless.

So far, 'ecstatic immanence' may sound acceptable. But a corollary of it is that the world of language, the dance of signs, is not anchored to or controlled by anything wholly external to it. It really *is* outsideless. The norms of meaning, truth, value and so on are all immanent. We evolved them. No Castle has decreed them: they are just our shifting improvisations. There are rules all right, there are goalposts, but life is such that as we play its various games the very playing of them gradually changes the rules and moves the goalposts.

Everything is fluid and transient, everything slips away: but we can nevertheless be grateful to those who have pursued their dreams of transcendence. They have done us a service. Modern humans have inherited a cultural world that is like Mr Badger's house in the *Wind in the Willows*, a vast warren of a place, excavated over many generations. It has long been so complicated, with so many rooms, that people have thought of trying to break out of it and learn what it looks like from the outside. But because it's an underground house it has no outside. It consists entirely of spaces opened up from within by its own inhabitants, with the result that all those who have tried to break through to the outside have succeeded only in enlarging the interior – to our subsequent benefit. Thus the misguided religious and philosophical ambitions of the past have left us a valuable stock of cultural resources, to be used now as we think fit.

The antirealist vision of life is a vision of the world and the self as being 'Empty', in the Buddhist sense. There is no core-self, and nothing substantial and enduring out-there. Time has an arrow: it is unidirectional – but there is no reason to think that Time as a whole is going anywhere, or that History is scripted. There is no great Goal towards which everything is moving, no side-of-the-angels to be on, and no authoritative point of view from which we can be certified that we did the right thing or that what we did will be remembered. There is no great Cause towards which we can make our contribution.

In the past we in the West got our sense that moral action is worthwhile from various myths. They promised us external validation for our good deeds. An independent authority would in one way or another endorse them, record them, and utilize them for the fulfilment of its own greater Purpose. Such an authority needs to be a sort of cosmic bank, offering secure storage and operating by unchanging criteria, if it is to give us the *security* we demand.

When all these myths are lost, however, we are compelled to return into our own lives and the here-and-now, and to find the strength to affirm the meaning and value of our own action as we act. Extreme short-termism, because we cannot appeal to History, or to the future or to any great tidal Purposive movement in things. Everything melts away. Value is not conserved: nothing is conserved. We cannot even be sure that our own moral standards will remain unchanged. The experience of the past half-century has been that moral standards change so fast that we feel ourselves to have been as it were several different persons during the course of our lives.

When in the mid-eighties I was asked to attempt a spiritual autobiography, I could find no moral standpoint around which I could unify my life. I have changed too much and – mercifully – have forgotten too much. I'm lost in the flux, a string of selves. There's my-life-in-the-living here and now, but there is no my-Life in the sense of a coherent completed whole taking shape.

That project failed, but in any case we need to forget, and the whole world needs to forget the past. Born in 1934, I was a child during the Second World War, the most intense and thoroughly documented concentration of dreadful events, infamous deeds and noble acts in human history. At the time it seemed that such things could never be forgotten. But now they are fading; and unexpectedly it's a mercy.

In 1941 the Nazi occupying authorities required the four directors of a Dutch bank to take an SS officer in plain clothes on to their staff, so that he could gather information about the financial transactions of their Jewish clients. Two directors refused and were shot; the other two agreed to collaborate, and were themselves shot at the end of the war a few years later. The person who told me this story, the grand-daughter of one of the men, left me a little unsure whether her own grandfather had been a hero or a traitor. It was all so long ago. The families involved still know each other, and do not particularly wish to be divided by the past. Grandfather died in the war, the younger generation have learnt, but what difference does it make now whether the precise year was 1941 or 1945?

I was startled at first by this forgetting, but on reflection I see that it was right. Too much remembering poisons the soul – and it is not necessary to quote examples. We can do without any Recording Angel or other memorialization of our lives; and, secondly, we don't need any higher Purpose, either. For to think that our action will not have worth unless it gets taken up into the fulfilment of some greater purpose than our own is in effect to hold that it is better to be a servant than to be a free person, which is incorrect.

The final argument that we need to deal with is the argument that my own judgment that what I'm doing is worthwhile is insufficient to sustain my confidence. I need moral endorsement or validation by a superior moral Authority, whose value-judgments are more solid, well-founded and enduring than my own. But here too there seems to be an absurdity. For I cannot consistently hold that it is better for me to do what someone else thinks I ought to do, than it would be for me here and now to do what seems right to me. Although Roman Catholic apologetics has made so much in the past of the argument that an objective authority is needed, it remains in fact an axiom of Catholic moral theology that conscience must always be followed. The axiom remains an axiom because it cannot be denied without paradox; for how could it ever be wrong for you to do what you conscientiously think to be right?

We can now draw the conclusion from all these arguments. The moral value of a good action does not need to be externally

confirmed, or remembered or conserved. No moral or onto-
logical support or context is needed. It is only for historical
reasons that we Westerners are alarmed by the thought of action
on the basis of Emptiness, action in the Void, action in 'mean-
inglessness'.

We can and we must act in the Void, and I say more: I say
that action in the Void is purer, cleaner and more beautifully
gratuitous. We Westerners still harbour a lingering desire for
'meaning'. The desire for our life to be meaningful turns out
under scrutiny to be a desire for independent moral endorsement, for memorialization and for incorporation into the fulfilment of a larger purpose than our own. It is a desire to return to
childhood, of course; but more seriously, it is a relic of the
former mass institutionalization of humanity within the old
realism. As such, it is something we must leave behind as soon
as possible. Especially between about the fourth and seventeenth
centuries, during the period of its strongest alliance with
platonism, our religious tradition taught us to dislike and to
shun the transient as corruptible and doomed. All value was
ascribed to the unchanging and purely spiritual Sacred realm.
Only traces of another attitude survived, as for example Jesus'
deliberate short-termism and his invoking of the lilies of the field
and the birds of the air. But as things now stand, our lingering
anxious desire for fictions of immortality, immutability and
absoluteness is itself the problem. True religion now consists
not in grabbing at such fictions, but in being cured of the
need for them. Selflessly to love the transient and let it go: that
is beatitude. Selflessly to stop clutching and let go completely
is to drop into a beatitude that was already waiting for us.

4

Active and Contemplative Religion

Language, I said, produces the world on its outer and subjectivity on its inner face, which makes possible the back-projected and metaphorical theory of the-self-in-the-world that has been proposed. Language is expressive, expression presupposes a 'body' and 'body-forces', and our human expressions betray a certain ambivalence. Continuing the analysis, we saw ambivalence as the effect in expression of disequilibrium amongst the body-forces, and then saw disequilibrium as having been implicit in the project of life from the outset. Biological theory itself assures us that evolution wouldn't have happened, and we would not be here, unless every organism struggles both for its own life, and for a mate; both to raise its young and to give place to them, and so on. More generally, the very transience of life, as a discharge of energy, is such that life and death, Eros and Thanatos, are oddly confounded. For is it not the case that the more ardently the flame of life burns in us, the more rapidly we are hastening to our death – as if vitality were the same thing as mortality?

So by regressive analysis a certain irregularity in the world was found to have given rise first to life, then to ambivalence, then to consciousness (which is the discomfort that a conflict of forces within it causes to the organism), and finally to anxiety-relieving cosmological stories and theories like this one, which complete the world by bringing it into focus and representation in language. So consciousness is the prime example of what Derrida has termed a *supplement*. It may seem to be a late arrival in the world, and something merely epiphenomenal. But it is more than that. It is a bit of superstructure that curves back in time to complete its own base.

There is then no sharp distinction between the world and our view of it. For us humans, the two are the same; and there's nobody else. The beautiful scientific world-picture that our restless discontent has elaborated can also purge our unhappiness, as we pass away into the world we made. There is creation and there is redemption: our dividedness finishes and unifies the world, and the finished unity of the world promises to heal our dividedness. Schleiermacher and Wordsworth began to describe this, and it has subsequently been called nature-mysticism, eco-piety and, here, 'ecstatic immanence'. It is as if one finds oneself blissfully disappearing into and drowning in the beauty of the visual field. Its order and brightness, its *consciousness*, is ours, is *me*. But the revelation here is not of any 'higher' truth at all. It is only my last and fullest acceptance of the simple fact that I am only a transient – and slightly discordant – collection of, and pattern of relations amongst, natural phenomena – or rather, 'sign-formed events'.

This, it should be said, is a sublime not of formlessness but of symbolic plenitude. Mark C. Taylor, writing about Barnett Newman's great painting *Vir Heroicus Sublimis* (1950–51) in the Museum of Modern Art, New York, links it with the Kantian dynamic sublime.[1] Kant regards the sublime as measureless, incomparable and even painful (*Critique of Judgement*, §§25–29), and associates the 'dynamical sublime' in particular with Nature's overwhelming might. Taylor then suggests that Newman, by producing a very large abstract painting which appears to engulf the spectator who draws near to it, has transferred the dynamical sublime from nature to culture.

Ecstatic immanence is different. One is not so much crushed or overawed as *melted* by sensuous and symbolic richness. Theories – and especially historical and developmental theories – now shape perception much more than they did even for Kant. Consider how, for example, a country walk is now a walk through geological history and economic history; and consider too how biological theory has changed the way we see animals and plants.

Ecstatic immanence, then, is a product of the great richness of modern theory. In the case of Barnett Newman's paintings, what makes his scarlet so gorgeous and dizzying is the intense evocativeness of precisely this colour. It starts up so many divergent trains of association that one feels dissolved. The self vanishes into the movement of signs which it is. Melting me into the flux of things, the painting recalls me to the sober truth – but in a way that is also a mystical experience.

So as our enquiry approaches the goal of completely naturalistic thinking, we find ourselves approaching also the goal of the religious quest. That is beautiful and Spinozist. But there's more yet. Language, as we noticed, does not produce just one great Subject, but an intersubjective and polycentric social world. To give an account of social action, we need first to explain how the social is produced.

We saw individual consciousness as produced by a certain disequilibrium and consequent ambivalence within the individual organism. Similarly, the social is produced by ambivalence in the relations between organisms. We have already suggested this, but we have not spelled it out; so let us begin from the familiar fact that to each individual another may be colleague or competitor, friend or foe, a permitted or a forbidden mate, attractive or repellent and so on. It is not hard to see the biological advantage here of a measure of ritualization of social interactions, to give to each organism the time to resolve its uncertainty and its mixed feelings in the presence of what we may call 'objective ambivalence'. Since perhaps long before Freud and Jung, psychology has seen the emotions as coming in paired opposites (love-hate, tenderness-violence, fascination-horror and so on). This 'subjective ambivalence' is reflected in our extraordinarily strong impulse to construct the world in terms of binary contrasts. I have in mind the contrast between two things or realms, each of which excludes the other, while yet each of which somehow presupposes, needs and remains locked to the other because it needs it for its own self-definition. Such contrasts seem to pervade the cultural realm, where normality always seems to define itself by describing and shutting out an abnormal Other to which it nevertheless remains secretly attracted. That is how it is with order and disorder, the natural and the unnatural, the law-abiding and the lawless, respectable society and the underworld, moderation and excess, the straight and the gay, virtue and vice, the settled and the footloose. To quote a contemporary example, even the most politically-correct person can seek an occasional moral holiday, an outburst of joyful incorrectness.

The secret, which perhaps only great art and strong poetry understand, is (again) that ambivalence made our world-building possible, and shapes the form it takes. Knowing this secret takes one into a region that morality cannot understand, because morality cannot accept the idea that it needs to include its own Other. But religion does so. In morality the return of the repressed may happen but is always unacknowledged, whereas religion very strikingly incorporates its own Other as a pet black sheep. It is not just that orthodoxy needs heresy for its own self-definition, but also that religion seems to have at its very heart a streak of excess or perversity. However hard it seems to be trying to set up a calm, disciplined and orderly social world, a touch of the Other keeps showing through. Blasphemy and sacrilege are never far away; Catholic art in particular keeps hinting at the forbidden.

Some commentators say (following St Paul) that laying down the Law creates the possibility of breaking it, and that every definition of normality cannot help but make transgression seem more enticing. The very act of erecting a fence at once makes the grass greener on the other side of it. Yes, yes: but the touch of perversion is hugged closer to the heart than that. A whiff of sadomasochism and even cannibalism colours Christian symbolism, piety and ascetical practices, and the church, the bride of Christ, is a blamelessly-respectable matron who makes no secret of the fact that she likes occasionally to take a large bite out of her partner.

Why? We have a clue here to explain how human culture, in its luxuriant and gratuitous excess, has become so very different from animal cultures.

When earlier we were discussing the symbolic exchanges of

seabirds during the breeding season we saw them as the fore-runners of our human language-games. Birds that may at other times be solitary, aggressive and rapacious have to become social during the breeding season, and must perform a lengthy and complex chain of behaviours in the right order. So the birds' ritualized symbolic displays serve in various ways to relieve excess nervous excitement, convey messages, order social relationships, and trigger off the behaviours appropriate at each stage of the breeding cycle.

Very well. Darwin himself saw clearly that the new style of explanation that he was inventing would in due course be applied to behaviour, psychology, and cultural symbolism. But how has it come about that in human beings the elaboration of language-games and cultural symbolism has been taken to such extraordinary lengths that it has by now circled back and engulfed the whole of the natural background out of which it emerged? How did Culture get to be so big that it ingested all of Nature?

So far I have suggested only that we are the most complex and afflicted of all creatures. We are organisms with many organs or subsystems whose various aims are often at cross-purposes. So we experience more ambivalence both subjective and objective, more inner pain, and therefore a greater need for expression and communication, than any other animal. Our dividedness betrays itself in our symbolic expression, in which others can easily read it. They feel for us and with us, and so a community of sympathy (Greek for compassion, co-feeling) becomes a community of consciousness. And it has been argued already that we humans are the first cosmological creatures. Being very divided, we are very restless, anxious and insecure. To relieve ourselves we have to be culturally very productive, surrounding ourselves with a protective cocoon of cultural symbols and myths. And precisely because we are so anxious and so aware of our own transience, we have demanded myths that are vast, cosmological and validating, in order to stabilize our values.

Yes, the illusion that we human beings need most of all is the illusion that our illusions are not illusions at all, but sacred and eternal verities. Nearly all of human life hitherto has been founded on the conviction that some little cluster of human traditions – customs, beliefs and values – is not just our own recent product, but goes back to the very beginning of things.

We now see the next step in the argument. What distinguishes the human scene is not just the fact that we are more complex, more divided, more afflicted, and therefore need to communicate more, with more vocabulary and in more language-games, but rather the fact that we humans have developed – and presumably *need* – so many secondary games, seemingly excessive or needless games, games about games. The secondary games often take the form of public performances, sporting, dramatic, and religious. They also include the proceedings of parliaments and courts.

Let us consider the structure of these 'meta-games'. They are supremely *public* performances. They are enacted within an enclosed space that is divided into three. There is the auditorium, gallery, 'stand', nave or whatever, in which the public gathers. Once they stood, but nowadays in the West we expect to find seating.

It is a very important matter of principle that the proceedings to be witnessed should as a rule not be held *in camera*, but should be public. So the presence of the audience is constitutive. They 'assist' just by their presence, but may also applaud, lend support, chant, sing or otherwise participate.

The second space within the outer enclosure is the floor, field, arena, stage, turf, platform or other space upon which the professionals act. This space is in the highest degree public, and therefore sacred: it is commonly framed or fenced-off in some way. The events that take place in it are social enactments. In some cases – weddings, votes or verdicts – permanent social change is brought about; but the common feature of all these public performances, sporting, artistic, religious, judicial and political, is that through them in different ways society represents itself to itself.

The third space is the backstage region from which the performance is produced or stage-managed. It includes dressing rooms or vestries, offices, stores in which stage-properties are kept, and the controllers of the lighting, backdrops and other machinery.

Interestingly, no special trouble needs to be taken to conceal the fact that the events displayed are stage-managed from a hidden region behind the scenes. Everyone knows that, but it doesn't matter. Only what is on show, up front, matters. Competent persons must follow exactly the right form in the proper place and in public; and then the act is valid *ex opere operato*, as theologians put it.

What we have here is action in the strongest sense, action that creates social reality. It is usually pictured as being irreversible, for only if in some significant respect the correct procedure was not followed can there be grounds for rerunning the race, declaring the marriage null and void, taking a fresh vote, or allowing an appeal.[2]

All these points are important and worth making because since about the time of Luther our Western individualism has so often led us to fancy that what we do as private individuals in private life is of more moral and religious significance than what we do as officials acting in a public capacity. But it behoves an antirealist to note that the reverse is nearer the mark. The true sanctum or holy place is not the inner life of the private individual, but rather, the highly-public space that has been specially-appointed for the performance of the rituals by which social realities are created. And action on the stage is not restricted to a small professional class of public persons. For all of us – for example when voting or marrying, or as officials or as paid-up members of parties and pressure-groups – make some contribution to the public sphere, and act in public space.

There is more to say. We have a very long tradition of interest in the ways in which individuals pursue personal growth and self-realization. 'Where Id was, there Ego shall be': the individual pursues the purest and clearest self-consciousness attainable. But society's struggle to represent itself to itself, and thereby to become conscious of itself and its values, through religion, through kingship, through its legal system, through art and so on, is older – and perhaps philosophically prior, too. The self-consciousness of society logically precedes the self-consciousness of the individual. It follows that, contrary to the traditional Christian and philosophical individualism, what we do as officials in our various vocations is prior to and more important than what we do and are as individuals.

There are points here that must be studied in detail, because our tradition has done so much to hide them from us. Philosophy, from Plato to Kant at least, extolled the rational individual who examined himself and his own life, who (with God's help, maybe) defined his own meanings and discovered the Truth for himself, and who was lucidly self-consistent in living the life of reason. Our tradition in spirituality and asceticism ran along parallel lines in its demand for strict self-examination and self-purification. The aim was to produce the same lucid consistency and singleness of mind in the living of the life of devotion. And our moral tradition likewise privileged strict *moralism*, the bringing of the whole of the individual's life under the rule of a rational system of moral law by which it would be guided towards its Telos or goal. 'Moralism' here means a strict consistency which refuses to acknowledge the Other or to grant any holidays.

However, the point of the stress upon ambivalence that has been running through these pages is that such a complete rationalization and moralization of life is not wholly attainable even at the individual level, and is out of the question at the social. Society, as they say, is 'a very broad church', the broadest of all. Wherever any line is drawn, the excluded Other still remains a part of the whole. And because society can never entirely banish its own Other, the repressed and excluded Other tends especially to return in those public performances, festivals and exhibitions, held in sacred, public arenas, through which society represents itself to itself. Thus it comes about that in trying to shift the focus of moral attention away from individual self-purification and towards the public sphere, we find ourselves coming up against the Other.

In brief, the argument is that the action of workers,

professionals, artists and so forth is public. It goes on in public space, is on public show and is publicly accountable. It cannot be blinkered. It must take account of and make provision for the Other. The individual may be narrow, but the public must be 'broad'. The Sacred *is* that breadth, which I think is why Georges Bataille insists that the Sacred is 'beyond good and evil'. To be the Creator, or the space in which everything is produced, the Sacred must include a touch of darkness, otherness, ambivalence and perversity – as the God of the Hebrew Bible does, thank God!

It is a very familiar observation that those narrow-minded and puritanical persons who wish to censor art are nearly always wrong. Great and life-affirming art is generous and celebratory. It is capable of including both saints and villains, both high life and low life, both the law-abiding and the lawless within its vision. It is big enough to recognize and to find space for the Other. Only recently have we begun to acknowledge that the same needs to be true of great religion. In the main tradition of Catholic Christian art there is abundant material which nowadays gives great encouragement to paedophiles, gays, and enthusiasts for sadomasochism. The faithful find this very disconcerting, but we can add that there is also a great deal of straight heterosexual eroticism: consider, for example, the sheer voluptuousness of Baroque religious art. In its late summer, Christian art became sumptuously this-worldly. In addition, both in biblical and in Christian doctrinal thinking, changes of status and value-reversals are very prominent, and all Christian societies know of festival times when the normal rules are suspended. In short, Christianity may like other faiths preach a double message. In its official voice it praises sobriety, reason, control and order: but *sotto voce*, in its symbolism and its art, it whispers of forbidden things. At its best, Catholicism was a magnificently public faith which professed to be, precisely, Catholic – i.e. all-embracing. So it is no surprise to find it (inadvertently, no doubt?) insinuating its own Other, and half-subverting itself by ingeniously combining eroticism with asceticism.[3]

We see then that both art and religion, in so far as they involve great public exhibitions and performances through which society represents itself to itself, must exceed morality. And if the sacred is supremely the public (i.e., that through which society is itself and recognizes itself), then there is an important sense in which the sacred is beyond good and evil.

This is a very unpopular idea, so let us hasten to explain it. Theology has recognized that God has a left hand as well as a right, a back as well as a face, and a shadow side as well as a shining side. Similarly, however society defines normality, it will always thereby create an Other, which nevertheless remains a part of it. So any truly comprehensive (equals sacred, equals public) representation of life in art or religion cannot help but allude to and even include its own excluded Other. Where art or religion achieve a vision that is truly redemptive or reconciling they will efface the lines of division and actively reincorporate the Other into the whole, even if the Other is life's sheer contingency, even if the Other is pain and death. The greatest achievement of active religion is therefore in the most public way to say the most resounding Yes to life in the face of the worst – and to hell with moaning about the so-called Problem of Evil, a problem that arises only against the background of a narrow and primitive theology.

Three visions of life. The typical Western vision of our life sees it as *libidinally-driven.* The energy that powers us is all the time seeking to come out into symbolic expression. It seeks to objectify itself and then joyfully to recognize itself in its own self-representation. In short, reproductive male sexuality is the model here: it is supposed that what we most desire is to create and project out a spitting image of ourselves. A man wants to see himself and recognize himself in his body of work, his achievement, his son; and through it he plans to cheat death.

So we aim to find self-fulfilment through self-expression. What I need is to be able to see myself in something I have made that will survive me. Perhaps the most successful exemplar of this ideal is the male Renaissance artist. But was there a faintly

absurd genital vanity in his relentless striving for heroic great-
ness of individual self-expression?

A typical Eastern vision of our life sees it instead as *founded in
Emptiness*. It sees the Western quest for self-realization through
self-expression as illusory. Why mistake an itch in the loins for
an immortal soul? What is this big Ego? This thing that I made,
identify myself with, and hope to survive in, is no more real and
substantial than I am. Did I hope to become real at second-
hand? I need to be liberated from the illusion of the Self. I need
to become still enough to allow empty, blissful, insubstantial
consciousness to realize itself in me. The 'centre' of the Self is
already waiting for us: it is just the empty, blissful blue Void that
is left when we are fully freed of all our illusions.

The third vision of our life sees it as *sign-driven*. It begins by
pointing out the danger of reifying Emptiness or the Void, as if
one supposed that the words name something out-there that is
blissful. In Derek Jarman's film *Blue* (1993), which consists
visually of nothing but a blue screen, the blue is not truly Empty.
It is a sign, as 'Emptiness' and 'the Void' are signs. So the true
emptiness is not to be significantly silent but to empty oneself
completely, going out without remainder into the transience and
the self-loss of communication. There is no real self: we exist
only in the temporal unfolding of our communicative relationships with others. So the true liberation is to give up *all* illusory
notions of immortality, whether within the world of signs or
out of it, and instead simply to say Yes to our own transience.
We dance away, we disappear into the Whole and are gone.

None of these visions of our life is True, but none is forbidden
either. All have been proved workable.

Most of our traditional moralities divided the world in various
ways between the actual and the ideal, is and ought, flesh
and spirit, and the manifest realm accessible to us versus a
mysterious and hidden but more-Real world-beyond.

I have rejected all such distinctions. There is only one world,
the manifest world, and it's all up front and all on one level,
with nothing hidden. Nothing is supernatural, esoteric or deep.

What I have said here differs just a little from the traditional Cartesian and scientific belief that the world is in principle completely knowable. René Descartes wanted to make everything fully transparent, either to pure conceptual thought, or (in the case of the material world) to mathematical thought. We differ from him in having rejected his mind/body dualism and in having dropped the self down into the flux of the world. My mental life (such as it is) is a flux of language-formed events, and the objective world is also a flux of language-formed events. So I have merged the former into the latter. Completely. And the language-formed flux is endless and has no outside. It is flat like the visual field, but we structure it and read it in depth. Nothing becomes manifest until a sign has in some way formed it. You may look at, but you will never *see*, anything that is completely formless: all our perception and apprehension is formative. To see something is already to have interpreted it; that is, to have encoded it in language.

What follows? Descartes and his successors wanted to make the world completely transparent to the mind, and to claim that we are capable of absolute knowledge. In principle it would seem that human knowledge can become as total and perspicuous as God's.

Our account here is a little different. We agree with the scientific programme: everything is in principle intelligible, everything is given to us, and nothing is mysterious – because what is given, the manifest world, is outsideless. However, we do not claim absolute knowledge: we say only that since everything is language-formed, everything can be as clear to us as language is – *but no more so*. It's all ours, it's about as clear as text is, it's about as clear or unclear as this book is.

As we turn now to ethics, it should be obvious that I propose a purely this-worldly and environmental ethic, one whose scope is as broad as the scope of language itself. It will be an ethic of life-affirmation, that will seek to say Yes to all the conflicts and the ambivalence of biological as well as just of human life. For the one cosmological distinction that has survived in our account is the distinction between the non-living and the living.

As we have noticed, current physical theory pictures all things as drifting apart and scattering away into dissolution and uniformity. In about 10^{30} years from now (if it hasn't imploded by then) the cosmos is going to be really *boring*. Living things, by putting up their local and somewhat anomalous resistance to this downhill slide have made the world, and in particular our corner of it, interesting. For the time being, anyhow.

In classical and mediaeval times thinkers assumed that life as such could be taken for granted. Indeed, it was often devalued, being regarded as merely the 'lower nature' that we shared with animals and plants. For us humans the important thing was not thus 'merely' to live, but to live well: and this living well meant preparing oneself to leave natural biological life behind altogether, in favour of eternal life and immortality. Our forebears were doubtless fortunate not to know that one day large tracts of the Earth would become so poisoned as to be almost uninhabitable, and mother's milk would be frequently reported unfit to drink. Now that day has come; and we are forced to see biological life itself as a value, and perhaps the first value. At any rate, it is the precondition for the attainment of any other values. We have to ask ourselves: 'What is the value of life? Why should we wish to live rather than not live, and why should we value biological life in general?'

In reply, I acknowledge that there is no value out-there absolutely. There is no 'objective' value. *We* make values: they are socially established, and they get written into our language-games. In the way they depend upon an ever-shifting social consensus, values are very close to meanings, so close that I have elsewhere defined a value as 'the feeling of a meaning'.

We are valuing beings because we are living beings, and a living being has an interest in life. Something is valuable to us in so far as it 'makes us feel more alive', and we warm to it. And, in addition, we must recognize that when we affirm life we commit ourselves to affirming it as it is and in its ambivalence.

From the previous generation everyone inherits, not just a language, but an established repertoire of language-games and therewith a complete world-picture. This will include a large and highly-differentiated stock of attitudes to and valuations of just about everything. I call this a valuation of life, on the analogy of a valuer who goes through a whole house assigning a value to every item. Culture's overall valuation of life assigns a very-delicately-adjusted feeling-response to everything, and thereby colours-up the world. Valuation of life, the system of meanings and world-picture are closely correlated, and are taught together.

So we always inherit a complete ethic and valuation of life, but because of historical change and our own restlessness we always modify it during our own lifetimes, exactly as we gradually modify the verbal usages that we were taught as children. Both values and meanings evolve continuously. Indeed, they evolve together.

Radically false metaphysical assumptions left over from the past lead many people to describe my ethical theory as being subjectivist or emotivist. But it is objective in at least three senses. *First*, what is valued is the whole life-world in all its aspects. As the objective world gets covered over with language, so it thereby also gets covered over with our valuations. *Secondly*, the ground of value is the fact that we are living beings with a highly-sensitive interest in life. Our evaluative response to things is not secondary or dispensable, but on the contrary is primitive. It colours up and differentiates our world for us. Valuation comes first. And *thirdly*, value runs alongside meaning in the way that its objectivity depends upon a public consensus that we confirm day-by-day and – perhaps – renegotiate day-by-day.

How then is moral change to be brought about? Short answer: by changing the valuations annexed to words as they are used day by day. As feminists and the members of various sexual, racial and other minorities know too well, moral change demands a long hard battle to bring about linguistic change, if something that presently has a dirty name is to be given a better name.

Moral action, then, must very often take the form of trying

to give something a better name, which means changing the ways certain words are habitually used, which in the long run must mean also changing the rules of the relevant language-games, which in turn must mean mobilizing public opinion and campaigning for changes in public policy. And that is why much of moral endeavour nowadays is channelled through single-issue pressure-groups that seek legislative change. A formal public enactment of the type we were discussing in the last section marks a moral victory, and seals a moral change.

Since on our account language covers over all the world, and all our world-building linguistic uses are matched to value-feelings, we see moral change as being usually very piecemeal and as happening along with linguistic change generally. Sometimes, though, a great writer, a strong poet, may use language in a revolutionary way. Startling new metaphors may change the associations of one thing with another that guide us in the construction of our world and the shape of our valuations. What makes the poetry 'strong' is that it carries with it a kind of inevitability. It is a little like *déjà-vu*: the words bring about a change that we now recognize as having been waiting to happen all along. In some such way strong poetry changes the past as well as the future, because it obliges us to rewrite the record in order to explain its appearance. And because of its world-making power and authority, strong poetry represents a continuation into our own times of the archaic pre-philosophical power of the Word.

Now, the Word has the power to destroy as well as to create. Strong poetry simply cannot be contained within the limits of the existing moral and religious conventions. It is a law unto itself, and may on occasion disregard, override or blaspheme against the rules. And this may be the right thing to do because (as we have seen) the Sacred is beyond good and evil and includes its own Other. To put the point in theistic terms, when evil seems triumphant and God's face is dark, there may have to be a paradoxical but unavoidable complaint against God in the name of God. In her distress, the believer finds that she has no option but to address her protest and cry for help to the very same One who has sent this senseless affliction. The expostulation has to be couched in the form: 'For God's sake, God!' So it is quite right, honest and intelligible that there should sometimes be a tone of bitter complaint, anger and blasphemy in the relation to God. In the Hebrew Bible this happens, as when Job and other sufferers address their protests to God in very violent language.

Do we see the point here? It is that because God includes his own Other (having a dark side, etc.), faith also needs to include a little bit of its own Other, in the shape of a touch of defiance, rebelliousness and *chutzpah*.

To that extent, those writers are correct who say that sacrilege and blasphemy are or can be valuable and productive forms of religious action that release the Sacred. And, more generally, just as in the age of critical thinking much or most of our moral action must question the existing valuation of life and strive to change it, so in the same way much or most of our religious action must question the existing religious order and strive to change it.

There was a time when people sincerely thought that religious action should be action that would please God by strengthening the church. But this merely increases somebody else's spiritual power and worsens the general state of religious alienation, so that religious action within the church ends up by being self-defeating. To be truly liberating, religious action must escape from organized religion, not strengthen it.

In summary, contemplative religion has been described as 'ecstatic immanence'. In it the self joyfully and even ecstatically accepts its own radical immanence in the flux of experience (or 'language-formed events'). It is a considerable achievement of culture that it has made some landscapes, some living things, some loves and some works of art so beautiful that they melt us, and we want to drown. It is enough to pass away into and to be part of all this.

Active religion is concerned with trying to make the world *that* beautiful. Its most typical expression today is the sort of pressure group campaigning that battles for the moral emancipation and enrichment of some group of people or some bit of the world. Nearly everyone can contribute something on that front. The sort of strong poetry that opens up new vistas is a great rarity, but is also to be cherished.

Once, Europe had a religion that taught us so to despise the body and the senses that one was glad to be freed from them. Life was valued so low that one was glad to find its end approaching. The profane world was regarded as being worthless.

We have travelled in the opposite direction, by suggesting that through religious and moral action the world can be made so sensuously beautiful that one is glad to pass away into union with it.

We should live as the Sun does. The process by which it lives and the process by which it dies are one and the same. It hasn't a care. It simply expends itself gloriously, and in so doing gives life to us all.

5

After All

I began by describing our present cultural situation as being both post-Christian and post-philosophical. Both traditional, ecclesiastical Christianity and mainline Plato-to-Kant philosophy subordinated the world of transient visible fact to a greater and more Real invisible world beyond. From this Real world above, it was claimed, you must seek the knowledge of what to think if you are to think aright and how to live if you are to live well. To gain this vital and saving knowledge of the Truth you must submit yourself to the authority of divine Revelation and of the church as its interpreter; or alternatively you must be schooled by pure philosophical Reason and learn to rise above the body, the senses and transience so that you can view the world and the human condition from the standpoint of eternity.

Historically, both philosophy and theology were thus 'realistic' in their orientation. Realism disparaged this world and postulated a Real World-above, an invisible world of eternal verities. Plato's philosophy was, in part at least, originally designed as a justification for the rule of lesser mortals by philosopher-kings, and the theology of church-Christianity – 'platonism for the masses', as Nietzsche calls it – was similarly developed as an ideological justification of clerical rule over the church. In fact, the task of realism is always the same: to justify the power and privileges of the élite who are the custodians of the currently most-prestigious knowledge-system. Nowadays metaphysical realism is at an end and theological realism, though still stoutly defended by the clergy, is clearly disappearing. Scientific realism, however, remains in almost complete control both of the scientific establishment and of public opinion. The vital, hard-to-win Truth about how things really are behind the veil of sense is now in effect identified with scientific theory.

I have tried to develop an antirealist vision of the world and the self, as a solution to the problems left by the demise of traditional realistic religious belief and philosophical thinking. The state of religious and intellectual decay and confusion into which we are now falling is so extreme that I have also wanted to argue that the only tolerably rational world-view-option left to us now is thoroughgoing naturalism. So I have attempted something rather way-out – a negotiated settlement between antirealist philosophy and the scientific world-narrative, to show that non-realism does not have to be anti-scientific.

I could even have been really extravagantly daring, and have argued back from utterance to the Big Bang simply by trans-cendental analysis. Looking back over the main heads of the argument, uttered language requires some sort of material vehicle to carry it, and takes time. Where there is utterance there must at least be a discharge of energies in time. Much or most utterance is in some degree ambivalent, revealing conflicting or divergent forces, both within the speaker and in the relations between speakers. This conflict of forces is then life's difficult, prickly struggle against, and protest against, the non-living background out of which it has emerged and upon which it feeds, and which must therefore also be conceived as a discharge and scattering of energies.

My wording at this point is cautious, and for a reason. In computer science it has been argued that there are no theoretical upper limits to the speed of computers. A logic-gate could in principle operate instantaneously, and without expending any energy; and if one gate might do this, then many might do so, in a way that preserved numerical succession without involving chronological succession. Thus it is theoretically possible that there might be a completed act of communication that did not involve any increase in entropy; a possibility from which it follows that I cannot argue transcendentally, and with the traditional philosophical necessity, that any act of communication whatever, in any possible world, must involve an increase in entropy. But I can counter-argue that my claim is valid for *utterances* and for the empirical world. And, I maintain, the theoretical possibility of instantaneous computation is just a limit-concept. It does the same job as the intuitive understanding of God does in rationalist metaphysics: instantaneous computation is to everyday computation as the intuitive Divine Mind is to discursive and finite minds. But the ideal limit-concept is not exemplified in the empirical world, and does not affect the present argument.

Along these lines, then, we might begin to show how to interweave antirealist philosophy and the scientific world-view. And there is more yet: for if in our language chains of signs form and clothe and thereby facilitate the discharge of energies, then we should see the objective world itself as waiting to be formed and made into an historically-developing Cosmos, in and by our description of it. Sign-formed, things can run sweetly. Articulation relieves *our* feelings and helps us to run smoothly, and in the same way the clothing of the natural world with scientific names and theories has made it smoother and sweeter to us. We tend to forget how fearful, suspicious and *unseeing* were the eyes with which people commonly looked upon Nature in prescientific times. Nature was savage and pagan, but now science has made it intelligible and interesting, even motherly, and an object of care and concern. Our ancestors sought redemption *from* Nature, but science has ingeniously solved that problem by redeeming Nature herself. Coupled with the increasingly biology-based understanding of human selfhood that has developed since about the time of Hume, a thoroughly naturalistic eco-religion now begins to look attractive.

However, in trying to sketch the antirealist view of life we must try not to look as if we are reinstating metaphysics and becoming systematic. Any systematic exposition of a topic is bound to look as if it is claiming to be the Truth. But I am not claiming that the antirealist view of life that I have sketched is True – nor can I dare to say that it is True that there is no Truth. I am saying only that the philosophy sketched in this book is true, at least for now. It is the point of view we would do well to adopt, because it is the one that works best. It makes the most

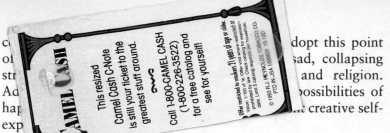

c... ...dopt this point
of ... ...sad, collapsing
str... ...and religion.
Ad... ...ossibilities of
hap... ...creative self-
exp...

Y... ...get a clearer view of what art, morality and
religion are all about. The traditional realism made morality and
religion into forms of servitude, assuring us, in Augustine's
words, that 'to serve is to reign'. Double-speak. And the same
traditional realism downgraded poetry and religious myth by
claiming that their function was merely to supply the common
people with tabloid versions of the pure conceptual Truth as
known to philosophers and to the saints in glory. Yes, realism
functioned to persuade you that you were a thoroughly second-
class citizen of the cosmos – which in turn made you gratefully
content with its metaphysical and religious consolations.

So you became locked into the system; a servant but a very,
very grateful servant. Now we can do better. Antirealism is
what the Enlightenment called our coming of age, and what
Jesus called the Kingdom of God. It is a state of complete
human fulfilment in this world, which has itself now become
a thoroughly humanized world.

Antirealism is completely naturalistic in so far as everything is
brought down to one level, and the self in particular is melted
down into the flux of the world. But the world as a flux of
language-formed events becomes a finished cosmos only in and
through our descriptions – and redescriptions – of it, descriptions which always express and involve also our feelings and
valuations. The Romantic poets and the nature-mystics were
therefore right, and much more right than they knew, to speak
of the harmony and the affinity that they found between the
world of Nature and the human heart. One continuous stream
of language constructs both the storm in nature and the storm
in my heart. The two are constructed together and in the most
intimate parallel – so intimate that when we are out walking
in a storm we feel the objective storm and the subjective one

as being in effect two faces of a single event. I cannot very clearly distinguish between the inside and the outside. Because we use language both expressively and descriptively, we tend all the time to spread our feelings over the world. Adjectives get transferred from us to things around us, as the chair becomes comfortable, the loaf healthy and the sea calm. The effect of this is that the inner world and the outer are a continuum, much as, when we are wholly immersed in music or work, the inner/ outer distinction simply disappears.

So much for the meltdown of the self in the antirealist vision of life. In art what happens is that the stream of signs seems to take on a life of its own. It becomes as-it-were spontaneously rich and productive, creating a small sub-world. Ordinarily the run of language, and the run therefore of language-formed sense-experience, and the construction therefore of the everyday world around us, is highly socially-disciplined. We are intensely amenable creatures, delicately attuned to each other, who all want to 'speak the same language' and therefore to make the same world in the same way. And the notable feature of natural science is that while the scientific community are busy extending and elaborating our common physical-object world, they are very careful to maintain the closest agreement with each other. Scientific knowledge is a community-possession which owes its strength to the determination of all to keep in step. Science has a passion for consensus and consistency. But art is more like dream or fantasy. It is less socially-controlled, more wayward. Within its 'frame' it makes its own temporary world-in-brackets. The art-product then does not add to our knowledge: its function is rather to refresh or to criticize mundane perception. It offers us a little sub-world that makes an oblique comment on the way we habitually construct our common world.

Now, if the common life-world were completely rigid, it might be difficult to see the point of this. But antirealism points out that it is only in and through our language, our feelings and valuations, and our theories, that the life-world becomes – and keeps becoming – finished and present to us. If we change our valuations, our feelings, our theories, and so our ways of describing things, then we change our world.

Throughout the two millennia or so during which metaphysical realism was dominant, the senses and our feelings were relatively disparaged. Only Reason counted. But from the antirealist point of view the education of the senses, of the emotions, and of our feeling for language, is a condition for our becoming capable of effective and world-changing moral and religious action.

Wholehearted and anxiety-free world-affirmation, not as an upper-class game but fully democratized, perhaps only begins to become thinkable during the last third of the nineteenth century. I mean, a cultural condition in which we humans are fully reconciled to the natural world and see ourselves as being wholly products of Nature, while at the same time the natural world has been made wholly friendly to us by having been exhaustively described and theorized by science. A cultural condition, I am suggesting, in which we no longer worry so much about the old binary contrasts between spirit and flesh, the Sacred and the profane, Culture and Nature,' reason and the passions, duty and inclination, soul and body and so forth. Perhaps the reason why 'reality' has come to an end, and the reason why our whole religious and cultural tradition feels as if it is evaporating, is that the old disciplines and constraints have finished their historical task. A time of fulfilment has come, and it is in many ways rather like the long promised 'Kingdom of God' hoped for by the rabbis of antiquity.

The old horrors, the four horsemen of the Apocalypse, still ride. But while ancient evils persist, there are also hopes such as no previous generation could entertain. A modern person can in principle be more fully reconciled to the world, to life and to death than the person of any previous period. That is a fulfilment.

So we have redescribed religion as a way of world and life-affirmation. Active religion was seen as a creative work of reimagining, redescribing and enriching some bit of the world; and contemplative religion, 'ecstatic immanence', was a dissolution of the self into the world thus made seductive and beautiful. Religion was always supposed to be a way of preparing for death and overcoming the fear of death, and I have argued that this can be done by making the world so beautiful that one could die content. But there is also a more general point. Truth needs to be *done*. A religion can be viewed as a way of practising, enacting and realizing a set of metaphysical doctrines. So I've tried to describe the emergence of new religious possibilities at the point where antirealism, post-Christianity and Kingdom-religion meet.

The story I have told has in one vital respect departed radically from the main religious and intellectual tradition. We have sided with Heraclitus (Fragments 214–222, in Kirk and Raven's numbering) and Nietzsche, the two teachers of the metaphysics of conflict. Everything flows, everything is produced by the interplay of conflicting forces, everything burns out and yet in its passing away contributes to the world's renewal.

The main tradition, by contrast, idealized a stable patriarchal order. In the beginning, in the Golden Age, everything was planned and ordered in a balanced and beautiful system by a single masculine intelligence or logos. There was no Otherness, no unconscious, no exclusion: *no argument*, as they say. But, you will remember, Woman started asking awkward questions and the divine order began to come apart. However, the hope is that one day we shall see it restored.

Perhaps every sort of theological and rationalistic vision of the world, every dream of the world as an intelligible and coherent system, is a dream of monarchy: the universal equitable rule of a single principle of order and harmony that makes everything make the same sort of sense. Inevitably, such a principle is thought of as masculine.

However, I've been suggesting that not only Darwin and Freud, but the modern world-picture generally, goes along with Heraclitus and Nietzsche in seeing the diversity of the world as the product of the interplay of opposed forces. Life struggles against the non-living, every living organism must experience some conflict of forces within itself, we human beings have produced our fabulously complex cultures because of our extreme need to find catharsis through symbolic expression, and so on. At every stage of the argument I have stressed the interplay of opposed forces both in nature and culture. The Same and its Other, conscious and Unconscious, positive and negative, male and female, life and death.

Ironically, I began by saying that we'd reinvent metaphysics as a network of unifying metaphors, the idea being to seek a view of life that might do justice both to what the Arts people are saying and to what the Science people are telling us. But we haven't ended up with even a metaphorical *system*: we have ended with the vision of a world, and a human life, endlessly at variance with itself. Heraclitus was right: conflict is built-in. That was Darwin's message, and Darwin was correct too.

So there was no Golden Age in the past, and there will not be any restored Golden Age in the future. But – I have argued – we can in retrospect see that it is precisely our own internal stress and ambivalence that has led us to develop around ourselves such a prodigiously rich and beautiful world as we now have. A world that we can be glad to live in, fight for, and die into. I'm talking about a post-contemplative kind of religion, which is a Kingdom-religion in the following sense. It aims completely to integrate the human into the world, and vice versa. We are world and the world is all ours. We made it, for we finish it as we appropriate it through language. And such a complete two-way reconciliation of humanity and world may claim to be a kind of fulfilment of ancient hopes.

Which leads me to stress in conclusion that in his own Kingdom-religion, Jesus of Nazareth did not envisage a peaceful restored Eden. On the contrary, the Sermon on the Mount throughout envisages the continuation of stress and conflict, persecution and suffering. But he promises joy in affliction: no more, but no less than that.

Notes

Introduction

1 Wittgenstein, *Investigations*, I.126.
2 *The Long-Legged Fly*, SCM Press 1987; *The Time Being*, SCM Press 1992, pp.15–20.
3 On this, see my 'The Last Judgement'; in Leo Howe and Alan Wain (eds), *Predicting the Future*, Cambridge 1993, pp.169–186.
4 T.J.J. Altizer, *Genesis and Apocalypse*, Westminster/John Knox Press 1990, pp.13–15.

1 *The Emergence of Post-Christianity*

1 Harold Bloom, *Ruin the Sacred Truths*, Harvard 1989, ch.1; (with David Rosenberg) *The Book of J*, Faber 1991.
2 J.A.T. Robinson, *Honest to God*, SCM Press 1963, p.18.
3 Albert Schweitzer, 'The Conception of the Kingdom of God in the Transformation of Eschatology'; reprinted in Walter Kaufmann (ed.), *Religion from Tolstoy to Camus*, New York: Harper and Row 1961, p.413.
4 See, for example, Geza Vermes, *The Religion of Jesus the Jew*, SCM Press and Fortress Press 1993.

2 *The Death of Tradition*

1 Jean Milet, *God or Christ?*, SCM Press 1961, ch. IV.
2 Ulrich Beck, the German sociologist, claims to have coined the term: see *Risk Society: Towards a new Modernity*, tr. Ritter, Sage 1992.

3 *How It Is*

1 Wilfred Cantwell Smith, *The Meaning and End of Religion*, SPCK 1978, p.72.

2 Locke quotes the phrase *tabula rasa* from Gassendi. In the *Essay Concerning Humane Understanding*, Bk II, ch.1, he himself uses the phrase 'white paper', in para.2. Locke goes on to represent experience as painting pictures on this white paper of the mind. But paper is also for *writing* on!
   Thomas Aquinas (*Summa Theologiae* 1a.79.2), using the phrase *tabula rasa*, attributes it to Aristotle.

3 *Three Dialogues between Hylas and Philonous*, 1713, the last paragraph. From this passage I have borrowed the image of a fountain, used later in the present text.

4 I acknowledge a debt to the late 'theological' works of Georges Bataille.

5 My argument at this point owes something to the 'radical empiricism' of William James's last (and posthumously published) writings. In the papers, 'A World of Pure Experience' and 'Does "Consciousness" Exist' (reprinted in *Essays in Radical Empiricism*, 1912), he is on the brink of making the linguistic turn. When it is made, what he is trying to say about the continuity of experience becomes much clearer.

6 *Metaphysics* Λ.

7 Good comments on this in Richard Rorty, *Essays on Heidegger and Others (Philosophical Papers Volume 2)*, Cambridge 1991, p.35, n.18.

8 Petrarch's letter is reprinted in E. Cassirer, *The Renaissance Philosophy of Man*, Chicago 1948, pp.36–46, from which my quotations are taken.

4 *Active and Contemplative Religion*

1 Mark C. Taylor, *Disfiguring*, Chicago University Press 1993, pp.88–91.

2 I am here indebted to the work of J.-F. Lyotard and Pierre Bourdieu.

3 On these matters, see for example, the bibliography in Peter Stallybrass and Allan White, *The Politics and Poetics of Transgression*, Methuen 1986. Theologians have so far been slow to join the debate, because they have found it difficult to recognize the ambiguity of their own language.

5 *After All*

1 See my 'Nature and Culture'; in Neil Spurway (ed.), *Humanity, Environment and God*, Blackwell 1993.

Index of Names